AF194400

Editorial

Touching distance on citizens' rights?

Why has the UK Government been so dilatory in scheduling Article 50 negotiations with the European Union? Messrs May and Davis insist the United Kingdom is keen to accelerate to make 'sufficient progress' in the eyes of the European Union, so that talks can progress to 'phase two' on the framework of future relations. Yet their tardiness in opening their diaries suggests otherwise, notwithstanding Mrs May's claim that an agreement on citizens' rights is within 'touching distance'.

One possible explanation may be found in the infographic opposite, tweeted by the European Commission early on the morning of Friday 20 October, shortly before the European Council agreed there had been insufficient progress to move to phase two of the negotiations. Headed 'BREXIT Citizens' Rights', it encompasses more than four million European citizens spread across the EU28 member states. To the left are 3.2 million 'EU Citizens in the UK' of whom two million are in employment. To the right are 1.2 million 'UK Citizens in the EU' of whom 0.5 million are in employment. Of course, these 1.2 million are also European citizens, at least until 'Exit Day', if and when the UK leaves the EU.

'Reciprocity' sits centrally in the infographic, meaning 'equal treatment' of both groups. How is this 'equal treatment' to be accomplished? Therein, perhaps, stands the 'stumbling block'.

Prominently displayed are two words, DIRECT EFFECT, with the accompanying explanation: 'as regards their rights, citizens rely directly on the Withdrawal Agreement'. The legal principle of Direct Effect enables individuals to immediately invoke a European provision before a national or European court. It is defined in these terms:

> The direct effect of European law has been enshrined by the Court of Justice in the judgement of Van Gend en Loos of 5 February 1963. In this judgment, the Court states that European law not only engenders obligations for EU countries, but also rights for individuals. Individuals may therefore take advantage of these rights and directly invoke European acts before national and European courts. However, it is not necessary for the EU country to adopt the European act concerned into its internal legal system. [source: EUR-Lex]

David Davis, the UK negotiator, spoke of 'direct effect if you like' at the end of round four negotiations. The relevant 'Joint Technical Note' comparing EU and UK positions on Citizens' Rights, dated 28 September 2017, gave a yellow light to 'individual enforcement of rights', noting 'UK to clarify'. The UK position was summarised thus:

> UK to incorporate the Withdrawal Agreement fully into UK law and ensure the UK courts can refer directly to it.

The EU position was more explicit.

> Directly effective provisions of agreement enforceable through the domestic courts of EU27 and UK (i.e. individuals can rely directly on Withdrawal Agreement provisions in front of domestic courts to override domestic implementing legislation).

Under the overall heading of 'Nature of the Agreement', there was no comparison of positions on the role of the European Court of Justice (CJEU). This thorny topic was 'for discussion in Governance Group'.

'Monitoring and oversight' are also for discussion in the Governance Group, as is 'future CJEU case law concerning the withdrawal agreement'. Positions were described. 'European Commission to monitor compliance,' according to the EU, while the UK position has two parts:

- Commission monitoring body for EU27.
- UK prepared to consider establishment of an independent monitoring arrangement in the UK.

Regarding ECJ case law, the EU position is:

> CJEU competence as per Article 267.

Article 267
Treaty on Functioning of the European Union

The Court of Justice of the European Union shall have jurisdiction to give preliminary rulings concerning:

(a) the interpretation of the Treaties;
(b) the validity and interpretation of acts of the institutions, bodies, offices or agencies of the Union;

Where such a question is raised before any court or tribunal of a Member State, that court or tribunal may, if it considers that a decision on the question is necessary to enable it to give judgment, request the Court to give a ruling thereon.

Where any such question is raised in a case pending before a court or tribunal of a Member State against whose decisions there is no judicial remedy under national law, that court or tribunal shall bring the matter before the Court.

If such a question is raised in a case pending before a court or tribunal of a Member State with regard to a person in custody, the Court of Justice of the European Union shall act with the minimum of delay.

The Spokesman
Touching Distance?

Edited by Tony Simpson

Published by Spokesman for the Bertrand Russell Peace Foundation
Ken Coates: Editor 1970 to 2010

Spokesman 137   **2017**

Subscriptions
Institutions £40.00 (ex UK)
£33.00 (UK)
£20.00 (UK)
£25.00 (ex UK)

A CIP catalogue record
for this book is available
from the British Library

Published by the
Bertrand Russell Peace
Foundation Ltd.,
Russell House
Bulwell Lane
Nottingham NG6 0BT
England
Tel. 0115 9784504
email:
elfeuro@compuserve.com
www.spokesmanbooks.com
www.russfound.org

CONTENTS

FSC
Mixed Sources
Product group from well-managed
forests and other controlled sources

Cert no. SGS-COC-006541
www.fsc.org
© 1996 Forest Stewardship Council

ISSN 1367 7748   Printed by the Russell Press Ltd., Nottingham, UK   ISBN 978 0 85124 868 4

European Commission

BREXIT
CITIZENS' RIGHTS

WHICH RIGHTS?

- ⋯ ⟶ Residence rights for citizens and their family members
- ⋯ ⟶ Workers maintain all rights (during employment and after employment, as jobseekers)
- ⋯ ⟶ EU students have the same tuition fees as UK students
- ⋯ ⟶ Economically inactive persons with sufficient resources can continue to reside
- ⋯ ⟶ Children have equal rights to education
- ⋯ ⟶ Coverage of health care expenses

More information: EU position paper: Essential principles on citizens' rights

- ⟶ Residents
- ⟶ Frontier workers
- ⟶ People covered by the social security system

- WORKERS
- SELF-EMPLOYED
- STUDENTS
- PENSIONERS
- FAMILY MEMBERS

EUROPEAN COURT OF JUSTICE (ECJ)
Uniform interpretation of Withdrawal Agreement

question on interpretation
preliminary ruling

UK COURTS
EU 27 NATIONAL COURTS
National courts request the ECJ to give a preliminary ruling, on the basis of which the national courts give final judgment

WITHDRAWAL AGREEMENT
Rights

DIRECT EFFECT
As regards their rights, citizens rely directly on the Withdrawal Agreement

EU CITIZENS IN UK
- ⟶ Total 3.2 million citizens (of whom 2 million in employment)

1000000
800000
600000
400000
200000
0

Poland
Romania
Ireland
Portugal
Italy
Lithuania
France
Germany
Spain
Latvia
Slovakia
Hungary
Netherlands
Bulgaria
Greece
Czech Republic
Sweden
Denmark
Belgium
Austria
Cyprus
Finland
Estonia
Malta
Croatia
Slovenia
Luxembourg

Source: ONS, 2015

UK CITIZENS IN EU
- ⟶ Total 1.2 million citizens (of whom 0.5 million in employment)

350000
300000
250000
200000
150000
100000
50000
0

Spain
Ireland
France
Germany
Italy
Netherlands
Cyprus
Poland
Belgium
Sweden
Denmark
Portugal
Greece
Malta
Austria
Hungary
Finland
Luxembourg
Bulgaria
Slovakia
Czech Republic
Lithuania
Romania
Latvia
Croatia
Slovenia
Estonia

Source: United Nations, 2015

- ⟶ Reciprocity: Equal treatment of EU citizens in the UK and UK citizens in the EU

The UK position is stated as:

> UK courts to be able to take into account the future CJEU case-law with a view to ensuring consistent interpretation.

No Joint Technical Note on Citizens' Rights was issued after round five of the negotiations, which ended on 12 October. We go to press before round six.

The EU's infographic addresses the unresolved issue concerning the European Court of Justice. Interestingly, it does not mention a role for the European Commission in monitoring and oversight.

In pursuit of 'uniform interpretation of Withdrawal Agreement', UK courts and EU27 national courts may 'request the ECJ to give preliminary ruling'. On the basis of this preliminary ruling, 'national courts give final judgment'.

In the EU view, uniform interpretation of the Withdrawal Agreement depends on the preliminary rulings of the European Court of Justice. This will achieve 'equal treatment of EU citizens in the UK and UK citizens in the EU', and thus establish reciprocity.

M Barnier summarised the position at the end of round five, referring to 'two common objectives':

- That the Withdrawal Agreement has direct effect, which is essential to guarantee the rights of all citizens in the long-term.
- That the interpretation of these rights is fully consistent in the European Union and in the United Kingdom.

> On these points, we will continue to work on the specific instruments and mechanisms which will allow us to translate this into reality. This means for us the role of the European Court of Justice.

The clock ticks, as Mrs May's government totters from one crisis to another …

Standing Up
for **Our Rights**

European Citizens' Gathering
Saturday 18 November ■ University of Nottingham

Our **Initiative on European Citizenship** opened for individual endorsement in May. *Standing Up for Our Rights: European Citizens' Gathering* will be an opportunity for those campaigning to uphold and defend the rights of all European citizens in the context of Brexit to engage, converse, co-operate, encourage endorsements of European Citizens' Initiatives and petitions, and plan future work.

Key themes will include upholding European citizenship, free movement (and beyond), human rights, children's rights, post-Brexit racism and xenophobia, the threat to workers' rights, and the consequences of Brexit on the wider political landscape.

Retaining European Citizenship Initiative *(see over)* and the Centre for the Study of Social and Global Justice at the University of Nottingham jointly host this gathering. The main component of the day will be a series of workshops and discussions organised by groups, organisations and individuals working on or conducting research on rights in the context of Brexit.

Speakers / Workshops:

Marina Pentroulis, University of East Anglia, spokesperson *Another Europe is Possible*
Suresh Grover and **Jagdish Patel** from *The Monitoring Group*
Andreas Bieler, *University of Nottingham*
Amelia Womack, founder of *Green Yes* and *Deputy Leader of the Green Party*
Matt Carr, *One Day Without Us*
Louise King, *The Children's Rights Alliance for England*
Elena Remigi, editor of *In Limbo: Brexit Testimonies*
Tony Simpson, *Retaining European Citizenship eci*
Claudia Delpero, editor of *Europe Street News*
Elizabeth Monaghan, *University of Hull*
Bakers Food and Allied Workers Union

TICKETS AVAILABLE VIA
www.eucitizen2017.org/citizens-gathering
£5 *waged* / **£3** *unwaged*

In Limbo

Claudia Delpero

Claudia Delpero edits Europe Street News, one of the best online sources for Brexit. When In Limbo *was published during summer 2017, she interviewed Elena Remigi, whose idea it was to collect Brexit testimonies of EU citizens in a book.*

EUROPE STREET
N E W S

With all the stories that appeared over the past 17 months on the plight of EU citizens living in the UK, it was only a matter of time before someone collected the testimonies in a book. The title is *In Limbo – Brexit testimonies from EU citizens in the UK,* which first appeared in June, with new revised editions due to be published by Byline Books in December 2017.

On 23 June 2016, the UK voted in a referendum to leave the European Union. That moment started a period of distress for EU nationals in the UK and for British citizens living in the rest of the EU. Their rights to study, work and live in another EU country, like any other European citizen, derive from EU Treaties and will cease to apply once the UK leaves the European Union. A solution might be found as part of the exit negotiations and the European Commission has put forward proposals to guarantee that nothing will change for these groups after Brexit. But there are areas of disagreement with the British government and there hasn't been any unilateral commitment to secure the rights regardless of the outcome of the negotiations. Hence living 'in limbo'.

The idea to gather the stories for a book came to Elena Remigi, an Italian translator who moved to Britain 12 years ago after living in Ireland and Canada. Véronique Martin and Tim Sykes, French and British academics, also joined the project.

'After the EU referendum people started to share their feelings in Facebook groups. They expressed grievances, sadness and a sense of betrayal. Brexit made a large community feel unwelcome in the UK. The emotional impact was strong, but people around us did not understand it. There are Europeans with British in-laws who voted to leave the EU without recognising this would deeply affect their family members,' says Elena Remigi. 'We wanted to show this human side of the Brexit story. If we only left the testimonies on Facebook, they would have got lost. We thought they should be preserved, shared and delivered to history.'

In Limbo includes some 140 stories of people who tell directly their experiences. Almost all EU countries are represented. There is a Dutch widow, who lost her British husband and does not qualify for permanent residence, although she has lived in the UK since 1967. There is a French mother who is ill and does not know if she can still rely on the British health system. There is a Romanian who remembers the Soviet Bloc and explains what borders mean to East Europeans. There are also British people married to EU nationals and British living in other EU countries, who voice their fears about the future.

The stories are grouped in five chapters, each representing a feeling: sorrow, disappointment, worry, anger and betrayal. There was little editing to maintain the authenticity of each testimony. Adding to the personal accounts, the Foreword is by the award-winning poet George Szirtes, a British-Hungarian who arrived in the UK as a refugee at the age of eight.

In total, almost 200 people sent their memoirs through the Facebook group 'Our Brexit Testimonies'. Those that didn't make it into the book are published online (ourbrexitblog.eu).

The purpose of the initiative is not profit, but awareness. The publication continues to be distributed to politicians in the UK and in Brussels. The first edition of *In Limbo* (£8.99 from Amazon) was self-published and the £6,000 needed to cover distribution and advertising was raised through a crowd-funding page. Proceedings from sale are used to support citizens' rights, says Elena Remigi.

She adds, 'when the UK triggered Article 50 of the Treaty starting the Brexit process, I described how I felt using some verses of Dante's Divine Comedy, Inferno.'

'Nel mezzo del cammin di nostra vita
mi ritrovai in una selva oscura
ché la diritta via era perduta…'

'Midway upon the journey of life,
I found myself in a dark forest,
for the straightforward path had been lost…'

She also recalls the final verses of Dante's Inferno:

'*E quindi uscimmo a riveder le stelle.*'

'*Thence we came forth to re-behold the stars.*'

'This is my wish for each one of us. Our limbo is not only about having the right documents or not. There is a psychological limbo too, in which we all feel we have plunged. My hope is that we can all return to behold the stars, content and settled as we first were before this referendum.'

www.europestreet.news
Claudia Delpero© all rights reserved

IN LIMBO:

BREXIT TESTIMONIES FROM
EU CITIZENS IN THE UK

From an idea by Elena Remigi

With a foreword by George Szirtes

Imagine… Imagine you left your native country because you wanted to explore your neighbouring world and embrace the European dream. Imagine you truly believed that the European Union was your home and that, as well as being a citizen of the country you were born in, you were also a citizen of Europe. Imagine you fell deeply in love with your new country. Imagine you built a life there, married, had children, a career, started a business…You felt happy and totally integrated.You were at home.

Then one day, your new country decides to vote to leave the European Union, which means that all the rules you have built your life on are going to change. One morning, after years and even decades, you suddenly feel unwelcome, unwanted, betrayed.Your certainties, your life and your security are gone.Your sense of identity too.Through no fault of your own, you are stuck in a painful limbo.

This is what has happened since the Brexit Referendum in June 2016 to the EU citizens who have made their life in the UK. This book of testimonies is their voice, their stories from Limbo, haunted by the poignant question: where is home?

Collected and edited by Elena Remigi,Véronique Martin and Tim Sykes

Cover by Gareth Harrey

Power Unplugged

Keir Starmer MP

David Davis, Secretary of State for Exiting the Eurpean Union and sometimes UK negotiator with the European Union, squirmed while Keir Starmer MP, his Labour opponent, filleted his fishy European Union (Withdrawal) Bill at Westminster on 7 September 2017. By turns, a governmental power grab that undermines rights at work and elswhere, the Bill also seeks to abolish the Charter of Fundamental Rights, which would be a huge blow against human rights in the United Kingdom. We reprint the Charter in full. Some relevant passages from the Commons exchanges are emphasised in bold.

'I beg to move, to leave out from 'That' to the end of the Question and add:

'this House respects the EU referendum result and recognises that the UK will leave the EU, believes that insisting on proper scrutiny of this Bill and its proposed powers is the responsibility of this sovereign Parliament, **recognises the need for considered and effective legislation to preserve EU-derived rights, protections and regulations in UK law** as the UK leaves the EU but declines to give a Second Reading to the European Union (Withdrawal) Bill because the Bill fails to protect and reassert the principle of Parliamentary sovereignty by handing sweeping powers to Government Ministers allowing them to bypass Parliament on key decisions, without any meaningful or guaranteed Parliamentary scrutiny, fails to include a presumption of devolution which would allow effective transfer of devolved competencies coming back from the EU to the devolved administrations and makes unnecessary and unjustified alterations to the devolution settlements, **fails to provide certainty that rights and protections will be enforced as effectively in the future as they are at present, risks weakening human rights protections by failing to transpose the EU Charter of Fundamental Rights into UK law, provides no mechanism for ensuring that the UK does not lag behind the EU in workplace protections and environmental standards in the future and prevents the UK implementing strong transitional arrangements on the same basic terms we currently enjoy, including remaining within a customs union and within the Single Market.'.**

The Secretary of State is keen to portray the Bill as a technical exercise converting EU law into our own law without raising any serious constitutional issues about the role of Parliament. Nothing could be further from the truth.

I will start with clause 9. As the Secretary of State and the Prime Minister know, the article 50 negotiations are among the most difficult and significant in recent history. Under article 50, the agreement will cover all the withdrawal arrangements and take account of the future relationship between the UK and the EU – a backwards look and a forwards look on something that might last for decades. We know that phase 1 will have to cover EU citizens, Northern Ireland, UK citizens in Europe and the money, and that phase 2 will cover security, cross-border crime, civil justice, enforcement of judgments, fisheries, farming, Gibraltar – you name it, we hope it will be in the article 50 agreement. We want it to succeed; we need an agreement. It will also include our future trading arrangements – hugely important – including any transitional arrangements, if there are any, and much more.

Arguably, the arrangements will extend to every facet of national life – not my words, but I will come back to them. The article 50 agreement will be voted on, but it will then have to be implemented. It is a colossal task likely to involve a host of policy choices and to require widespread changes to our law – on any view. So how will that be done? Enter clause 9:

> 'A Minister of the Crown may by regulations make such provision as the Minister considers appropriate for the purposes of implementing the withdrawal agreement if the Minister considers that such provisions should be in force on or before exit day.'

It is very likely to have to be in force before exit day, because otherwise there will be a gap, so that means the whole of the agreement, including transitional measures, being implemented under clause 9. It cannot be implemented after exit day, otherwise there will be a gap.

Let us be clear about how widely clause 9 is drawn. We have had some discussion about Henry VIII. Subsection (2) states:

> 'Regulations under this section may make any provision that could be made by an Act of Parliament' – it is a true Henry VIII clause; it can modify Acts of Parliament – '(including modifying this Act).'

The delegated legislation can amend the primary Act itself. That is as wide as any provision I have ever seen.

What are the limits and safeguards? Under clause 9(3), the regulations may not impose taxation, make retrospective provisions – they are usually a very bad idea – create a criminal offence or amend the Human Rights

Act. Everything else is on limits under clause 9.

Given that the clause is drawn so widely, one would expect an enhanced procedure or some other safeguards – surely not just ordinary old delegated legislation.

What are the procedures? Are they enhanced? No. The opposite. Part 2 of schedule 7 deals with clause 9. It makes it clear that unless the delegated legislation creates a public authority, or the function of a public authority, affects a criminal offence or affects a power to make legislation, it is to be dealt with by – what? The negative procedure for statutory instruments, which means the least possible scrutiny: it means that the widest possible power, with no safeguards, will be channelled into the level of least scrutiny.

That is absolutely extraordinary. Let us be clear about what it means, because I am sure that the Secretary of State and others will say that notwithstanding the number of statutory instruments for which the schedule provides, they can be called up and annulled, and Parliament will have its say. I looked up the last time a negative-procedure statutory instrument had been annulled in the House, and it was 38 years ago. I do not know how many Members have been in the House for 38 years, but many of us will not have had that opportunity. So much for 'taking back control'.

There is no point in the Secretary of State or the Prime Minister saying, 'We would not use these powers: take our assurance.' If they would not use them, they are unnecessary, and if they are unnecessary they should not be put before the House for approval today.

Clause 7, 'Dealing with deficiencies arising from withdrawal', takes the same approach as clause 9, as does clause 8, 'Complying with international obligations'. All those provisions are channelled into the negative procedure with the least possible scrutiny: they constitute a giant sidestep from parliamentary scrutiny on the most important issues of our day. But let me top it off. If you think that is bad – and I do – try clause 17. Subsection (1) states:

> 'A Minister of the Crown may by regulations make such provision as the Minister considers appropriate in consequence of this Act.'

So anything in consequence of the Act can be done under clause 17. Again, this is a proper, robust Henry VIII provision. Let us look at subsection (2). It states:

> 'The power to make regulations under subsection (1) may…be exercised by modifying any provision made by or under an enactment.'

That means amending primary legislation. In case anyone is in doubt, subsection (3) states:

> 'In subsection (2) "enactment" does not include primary legislation passed or made after the end of the Session in which this Act is passed.'

So the Government can amend any legislation whatsoever – primary legislation – including legislation in this Session. Everything in the Queen's Speech that is coming down the track could be amended by delegated legislation under clause 17. I have never come across such a wide power, although I have come across consequential powers. The Secretary of State will no doubt point to other statutes that provide for not dissimilar powers; I have looked at them, but I have never seen one as wide as this.

Members should not just take my word for it. A minute ago, the Secretary of State said that no one could suggest that this was a legislative blank cheque for the Government. Let me read out what has been said by the Hansard Society – not a political body, not the Opposition, but the Hansard Society – about clause 17.

> 'Such an extensive power is hedged in by the fact that any provision must somehow relate to withdrawal from the EU, but given that this will arguably extend to every facet of national life, if granted it would, in effect, hand the government a legislative blank cheque.'

Those are the words of the Hansard Society.

What is the scope and extent of that legislative blank cheque? How many pieces of delegated legislation are we concerned with? As the Secretary of State said, the White Paper suggested that there would be between 800 and 1,000, the vast majority of which would be dealt with via the negative procedure route. I do not think that the White Paper could, or did, take into account the further instruments necessary to implement the withdrawal agreement, but there could be very many more – well over 1,000 pieces of delegated legislation, given the least possible scrutiny.

I was glad to see that the Prime Minister was here earlier. Yesterday, during Prime Minister's Question Time, she told the House that 'the approach' – the Government's approach to the Bill – 'has been endorsed by the House of Lords Constitution Committee.'

I read the report again last night, and I have doubts about that endorsement.

As the Prime Minister and the Secretary of State will know, this morning the House of Lords published a further report on the Bill, which reached the following conclusion:

'The executive powers conferred by the Bill are unprecedented and extraordinary and raise fundamental constitutional questions about the separation of powers between Parliament and Government.'

The report – published by the Committee that the Prime Minister prayed in aid yesterday – went on to say:

'The number, range and overlapping nature of the broad delegated powers…would fundamentally challenge the constitutional balance of powers between Parliament and Government and would represent a significant – and unacceptable – transfer of legal competence.'

Far from being an endorsement, that is an explicit and damning criticism of the Government's approach.

Interventions
… It is not as if this point is being made for the first time today: these are the points that have been made since the White Paper was published – the moment we dealt with it. That was in March, the Bill was published in July, and there have been numerous reports since then, and I raised at the time the significant issues I am raising now, and there has been no move from the Government.

Chris Bryant (Labour)
The key point about clause 9 is that the Government have asked Parliament to allow them to alter the Bill themselves by secondary legislation once it has been enacted. If we look through the history of the 20th century, we will not find a single Bill that has ever sought to do that – not in time of war and not in time of civil emergency. In fact, every single emergency powers Act has expressly said that there shall not be a power for Ministers to alter primary legislation.

… Keir Starmer
I am on my feet answering the last intervention, which powerfully makes the point that this Bill is unprecedented in its scope. That is significant because the Secretary of State will point to some of the safeguards under the Bill for the exercise of some of these powers, but if delegated legislation can amend the Bill's powers once enacted then notions of exit day, how far the delegated legislation goes and which procedures are used could be amended by the delegated legislation. So it is a very real point.

… **Let me turn from parliamentary involvement to the protection of rights**. Many rights and protections derived from the EU are protected in delegated legislation under the European Communities Act 1972. Because they are underpinned by EU provisions, they have enjoyed **enhanced protection** – 44 years' worth. **They include some very important rights: the working time rights of people at work; the rights of part-time and fixed-term workers; the transfer of undertakings provision, which affects everybody who is at work if their company is taken over, so that their contracts are preserved, which is something we all believe in; and all health and safety provisions have been handled by delegated legislation under the 1972 Act, too.** It did not matter that it was just delegated legislation, because they had enhanced protection because of the 1972 Act and our membership of the EU. **The same is equally true of important environmental rights and protections for consumers.** Under this Bill, the Secretary of State says they survive, and I accept that, and he does have a commitment to rights at work, but **they do not survive with their enhanced status**; they survive only in delegated form. **From the date of this Bill, they are amendable by delegated legislation. All of those rights at work, environmental provisions and consumer rights are unprotected from delegated legislation.**

Victoria Atkins (Conservative)
On health and safety protections, the right hon. and learned Gentleman knows, of course, that there is a 1974 statute – the Health and Safety at Work etc. Act 1974 – which gives not just employees safety protections, but members of the public who are affected by conditions in the workplace. Surely that in itself acts as the primary protection to workers in this country under health and safety provisions?

Keir Starmer
No, I am afraid it does not. The Manual Handling Operations Regulations 1992, the Management of Health and Safety at Work Regulations 1999 and the Workplace (Health, Safety and Welfare) Regulations 1992 all post-date that, and in any event that does not deal with all the other rights I have mentioned.

Caroline Lucas (Green)
The right hon. and learned Gentleman is making an excellent speech. On environmental standards, does he agree that there is another problem – a governance gap? With the lack of the European Court of Justice and the

Commission, there is nothing to enforce those environmental standards, and therefore we need a new legal architecture; judicial review is not enough.

I am very grateful for that intervention, because one thing that is not on the face of the Bill is any enforcement provision for rights currently enforced in one or other way through EU institutions, or even reporting obligations. It is fair to say that there is the provision in the Bill for the creation of public authorities – by, guess what, delegated legislation – and maybe that could be used for remedies, but it is by no means clear on the face of the Bill, and that is an important deficiency.

Let me complete this point: does it matter that these rights have lost their enhanced protection? Yes, it does. Taking back control obviously carries with it that this Parliament can change those rights, as the Secretary of State rightly set out, but this is to change them by delegated legislation, not primary legislation; that is an important distinction.

Does it matter? Would anybody have a go – surely not in the 21st century? Well, in June 2014 the current Foreign Secretary called for an end to 'back-breaking' employment regulations, specifically the collective redundancies directive. The current International Development Secretary during the referendum campaign called for the Government to halve the amount of protection given to British workers after Brexit. And the International Trade Secretary – I am addressing the question of whether it is conceivable that a Conservative Government might change this; I am reading out the statements of three Cabinet members. In February 2012 the International Trade Secretary … wrote:

> 'To restore Britain's competitiveness we must begin by deregulating the labour market. Political objections must be overridden. It is too difficult to hire and fire and too expensive to take on new employees. It is intellectually unsustainable to believe that workplace rights should remain untouchable while output and employment are clearly cyclical.'

The Secretary of State for Exiting the European Union has a proud record on human rights and protections of people at work, but these are the statements of Cabinet colleagues, and this power in this Bill allows these rights to be overridden by delegated legislation.

Intervention

… I was suggesting that workplace rights, environmental rights and consumer rights should only be capable of being taken away by primary legislation. If there is any doubt, I can assure the hon. Gentleman that when I say primary legislation I mean legislation in this House; I thought that was taken as read.

Nicky Morgan (Conservative)
Does not the last intervention point to the fundamental misunderstanding that some have about this Bill – and I am afraid the Secretary of State mentioned it earlier? The point is whether the UK is going to become a rule-taker rather than a rule-maker. Our membership of the European Union has allowed us to influence the directives and regulations which have then been taken on board in this House and through our laws. What we are doing in this Bill – I will expand on this in my remarks – is not repealing, but reintroducing European legislation into this country, contrary to the intentions of those who wanted to leave the European Union.

Keir Starmer
I am grateful for that intervention and agree with it. May I move on to other rights, because they are dealt with more severely? Clause 5(4) singles out the Charter of Fundamental Rights for extinction. There are thousands of provisions that are being converted into our law and will have to be modified in some cases to arrive in our law, but only one provision in the thousands and thousands has been singled out for extinction – the Charter of Fundamental Rights. As the right hon. and learned Member for Beaconsfield (Dominic Grieve) argued in an article published yesterday, the principles of the charter provide 'essential safeguards for individuals and businesses'. That has been particularly important in the fields of Lesbian, Gay, Bisexual and Transgender (LGBT) rights, children's rights and the rights of the elderly.

The Secretary of State asks why this matters. I have here the High Court judgment in the case of David Davis MP, Tom Watson MP and others the Secretary of State for the Home Department. This was in 2015, when the present Prime Minister was Home Secretary. David Davis the Back Bencher was bringing to court the now Prime Minister. He will recall that he was challenging the provisions of the Data Retention and Investigatory Powers Act 2014. He was concerned that they would impinge on the ability of MPs to have confidential communications from their constituents. He continued to make that point in debates that we were having a year or two ago. In his argument, he cited the Charter. His lawyers made the argument that the Charter was important because it went further than the European Convention on Human Rights and therefore provided added protection.

I will not read out paragraph 80 of the judgment, although I am sure that the Secretary of State is familiar with it. As he knows, the Court found in his favour – he was right: the Charter did enhance his rights – and rejected the arguments of Mr Eadie, the distinguished QC representing the then Home Secretary, now the Prime Minister. So when the Secretary of State asks whether this move will make any difference, the answer is yes. We can see that from his case. I suspect that if he were still on the Back Benches, he would now be talking to me and others over a cup of coffee about how we should fiercely oppose clause 5(4) and ensure that it came out of the Bill.

Dominic Grieve (Conservative)
The right hon. and learned Gentleman makes an important point. Reading the mind of my right hon. Friend the Secretary of State, I think he asked why this mattered because he would insist that the general principles of EU law being preserved would replace the Charter. However, if they are not justiciable because we do not found a cause of action in our courts, the ability to assert those rights would evaporate.

Keir Starmer
That is exactly the point that was made earlier. To say that the changes do not matter because we can find that right elsewhere, but then to remove the right to do anything about an effective remedy, would mean that the exercise had achieved absolutely nothing … I spent 20-plus years as a human rights lawyer interpreting and applying provisions such as the Charter and acting for many people to whose lives it made a real difference, as the Secretary of State will know.

I want to move on the question of devolved powers. At the moment, EU law limits the powers of the devolved institutions. On withdrawal, the default position ought to be that the devolved institutions would have power over matters falling within the devolved fields, but clause 11 prevents that and diverts powers that ought to go to Edinburgh, Cardiff or Belfast to London, where they are to be hoarded. That is fundamentally the wrong approach, but it is totally consistent with the Government's approach of grabbing powers and avoiding scrutiny.

On that topic, let me deal with **exit day**, a crucially important day in the Bill. It is the day on which the European Communities Act will be repealed. **It is also the day on which the role of the European Court of**

Justice will be extinguished in our law, and that matters hugely, whatever anyone's long-term view, particularly for transitional arrangements. I heard the Secretary of State say this morning that he wanted transitional arrangements that were as close as possible to the current arrangements. I think he knows, in his heart of hearts, that that will almost certainly involve a role for the European Court of Justice – although he will say that it would be temporary.

Exit day, the day on which the role of the Court is extinguished, is crucial. Without it, we might not be able to transition on the terms that the Secretary of State was suggesting this morning. He knows that. Control over exit day is therefore hugely important. Who will have that control? People talk about bringing back control, and they might think that Parliament would have control over this important issue. But no. Enter clause 14, which states that

'"exit day" means such day as a Minister of the Crown may by regulations appoint.'

This will be in the sole power of a Minister. Anyone simply passing this Bill must be prepared to be a spectator on the question of what the transitional measures should be and how they operate. That is a huge risk to our national interests.

Wes Streeting (Labour)
The Secretary of State said earlier that it was 'silly' of me to raise the transitional arrangements in relation to our continuing to be in the single market and the customs union. If the Bill is enacted and we are outside the purview of the ECJ and not subject to EU law, we will effectively be ruling out membership of the single market and the customs union during the transition. How will that bring stability and certainty to British businesses? Why is this provision in the Bill?

Keir Starmer
This is the conundrum that the Secretary of State and the Bill have created. If exit day is in March 2019, it is difficult to see how we could transition on terms similar to those we are now on. What could we do? We could choose to push exit day two years down the line. No? Well, if we did not do that, but we recognised that the ECJ was necessary to the process, we would end up repealing what was once this repeal Bill, only to have to bring it back in again. That is the extent of the absurdity of the powers in the Bill.

Joanna Cherry (Scottish National Party)

The right hon. and learned Gentleman is making an outstandingly concise and forensic speech dissecting the difficulties in the Bill. He has drawn our attention to the problem with the definition of 'exit day'. Does not that problem also feed into the delegated legislative powers? Clause 7(7) states that Ministers cannot make regulations 'after the end of the period of two years beginning with exit day'. If exit day is going to disappear down the line, as the shadow Secretary of State has suggested, would not the power to make delegated legislation continue for even longer than the Government are now proposing?

Keir Starmer

It certainly could. The only way out of that would be to have multiple exit days. Members might think I am joking, but someone who drafted the Bill has thought of that, and it is conceivable that there could be multiple exit days, all chosen by a Minister and not by Parliament. The combined effect of the Bill's provisions would be to reduce MPs to spectators as power pours into the hands of Ministers and the Executive. This is an unprecedented power-grab – 'rule by decree' is not a mis-description – and an affront to Parliament and to accountability. The name of the Bill was changed from the great repeal Bill to the European Union (Withdrawal) Bill. The word 'great' should have been preserved, however. The title should have been changed to the great power grab Bill. Labour voted for the article 50 legislation, because we accept the referendum result. As a result, the UK is leaving the EU. That we are leaving is settled. How we leave is not. This Bill invites us to surrender all power and influence over that question to the Government and to Ministers. That would betray everything that we are sent here to do. Unless the Government make very significant concessions before we vote on Monday, Labour has tabled a reasoned amendment and will vote against the Bill.

Source: Hansard

CHARTER OF FUNDAMENTAL RIGHTS
OF THE EUROPEAN UNION

(2000/C 364/01)

Preamble

The peoples of Europe, in creating an ever closer union among them, are resolved to share a peaceful future based on common values.

Conscious of its spiritual and moral heritage, the Union is founded on the indivisible, universal values of human dignity, freedom, equality and solidarity; it is based on the principles of democracy and the rule of law. It places the individual at the heart of its activities, by establishing the citizenship of the Union and by creating an area of freedom, security and justice.

The Union contributes to the preservation and to the development of these common values while respecting the diversity of the cultures and traditions of the peoples of Europe as well as the national identities of the Member States and the organisation of their public authorities at national, regional and local levels; it seeks to promote balanced and sustainable development and ensures free movement of persons, goods, services and capital, and the freedom of establishment.

To this end, it is necessary to strengthen the protection of fundamental rights in the light of changes in society, social progress and scientific and technological developments by making those rights more visible in a Charter.

This Charter reaffirms, with due regard for the powers and tasks of the Community and the Union and the principle of subsidiarity, the rights as they result, in particular, from the constitutional traditions and international obligations common to the Member States, the Treaty on European Union, the Community Treaties, the European Convention for the Protection of Human Rights and Fundamental Freedoms, the Social Charters adopted by the Community and by the Council of Europe and the case-law of the Court of Justice of the European Communities and of the European Court of Human Rights.

Enjoyment of these rights entails responsibilities and duties with regard to other persons, to the human community and to future generations.

The Union therefore recognises the rights, freedoms and principles set out hereafter.

Chapter I
DIGNITY

Article 1
Human dignity

Human dignity is inviolable. It must be respected and protected.

Article 2
Right to life

1. Everyone has the right to life.
2. No one shall be condemned to the death penalty, or executed.

Article 3
Right to the integrity of the person

1. Everyone has the right to respect for his or her physical and mental integrity.
2. In the fields of medicine and biology, the following must be respected in particular:
– the free and informed consent of the person concerned, according to the procedures laid down by law,
– the prohibition of eugenic practices, in particular those aiming at the selection of persons,
– the prohibition on making the human body and its parts as such a source of financial gain,
– the prohibition of the reproductive cloning of human beings.

Article 4
Prohibition of torture and inhuman or degrading treatment or punishment

No one shall be subjected to torture or to inhuman or degrading treatment or punishment.

Article 5
Prohibition of slavery and forced labour

1. No one shall be held in slavery or servitude.
2. No one shall be required to perform forced or compulsory labour.
3. Trafficking in human beings is prohibited.

Chapter II
FREEDOMS

Article 6
Right to liberty and security

Everyone has the right to liberty and security of person.

Article 7
Respect for private and family life

Everyone has the right to respect for his or her private and family life, home and communications.

Article 8
Protection of personal data

1. Everyone has the right to the protection of personal data concerning him or her.
2. Such data must be processed fairly for specified purposes and on the basis of the consent of the person concerned or some other legitimate basis laid down by law. Everyone has the right of access to data which has been collected concerning him or her, and the right to have it rectified.
3. Compliance with these rules shall be subject to control by an independent authority.

Article 9
Right to marry and right to found a family

The right to marry and the right to found a family shall be guaranteed in accordance with the national laws governing the exercise of these rights.

Article 10
Freedom of thought, conscience and religion

1. Everyone has the right to freedom of thought, conscience and religion. This right includes freedom to change religion or belief and freedom, either alone or in community with others and in public or in private, to manifest religion or belief, in worship, teaching, practice and observance.
2. The right to conscientious objection is recognised, in accordance with the national laws governing the exercise of this right.

Article 11
Freedom of expression and information

1. Everyone has the right to freedom of expression. This right shall include freedom to hold opinions and to receive and impart information and ideas without interference by public authority and regardless of frontiers.
2. The freedom and pluralism of the media shall be respected.

Article 12
Freedom of assembly and of association

1. Everyone has the right to freedom of peaceful assembly and to freedom of association at all levels, in particular in political, trade union and civic matters, which implies the right of everyone to form and to join trade unions for the protection of his or her interests.
2. Political parties at Union level contribute to expressing the political will of the citizens of the Union.

Article 13
Freedom of the arts and sciences

The arts and scientific research shall be free of constraint. Academic freedom shall be respected.

Article 14
Right to education

1. Everyone has the right to education and to have access to vocational and continuing training.
2. This right includes the possibility to receive free compulsory education.
3. The freedom to found educational establishments with due respect for democratic principles and the right of parents to ensure the education and teaching of their children in conformity with their religious, philosophical and pedagogical convictions shall be respected, in accordance with the national laws governing the exercise of such freedom and right.

Article 15
Freedom to choose an occupation and right to engage in work

1. Everyone has the right to engage in work and to pursue a freely chosen or accepted occupation.

2. Every citizen of the Union has the freedom to seek employment, to work, to exercise the right of establishment and to provide services in any Member State.
3. Nationals of third countries who are authorised to work in the territories of the Member States are entitled to working conditions equivalent to those of citizens of the Union.

Article 16
Freedom to conduct a business

The freedom to conduct a business in accordance with Community law and national laws and practices is recognised.

Article 17
Right to property

1. Everyone has the right to own, use, dispose of and bequeath his or her lawfully acquired possessions. No one may be deprived of his or her possessions, except in the public interest and in the cases and under the conditions provided for by law, subject to fair compensation being paid in good time for their loss. The use of property may be regulated by law in so far as is necessary for the general interest.
2. Intellectual property shall be protected.

Article 18
Right to asylum

The right to asylum shall be guaranteed with due respect for the rules of the Geneva Convention of 28 July 1951 and the Protocol of 31 January 1967 relating to the status of refugees and in accordance with the Treaty establishing the European Community.

Article 19
Protection in the event of removal, expulsion or extradition

1. Collective expulsions are prohibited.
2. No one may be removed, expelled or extradited to a State where there is a serious risk that he or she would be subjected to the death penalty, torture or other inhuman or degrading treatment or punishment.

Chapter III
EQUALITY

Article 20
Equality before the law

Everyone is equal before the law.

Article 21
Non-discrimination

1. Any discrimination based on any ground such as sex, race, colour, ethnic or social origin, genetic features, language, religion or belief, political or any other opinion, membership of a national minority, property, birth, disability, age or sexual orientation shall be prohibited.
2. Within the scope of application of the Treaty establishing the European Community and of the Treaty on European Union, and without prejudice to the special provisions of those Treaties, any discrimination on grounds of nationality shall be prohibited.

Article 22
Cultural, religious and linguistic diversity

The Union shall respect cultural, religious and linguistic diversity.

Article 23
Equality between men and women

1. Equality between men and women must be ensured in all areas, including employment, work and pay.
2. The principle of equality shall not prevent the maintenance or adoption of measures providing for specific advantages in favour of the under-represented sex.

Article 24
The rights of the child

1. Children shall have the right to such protection and care as is necessary for their well-being. They may express their views freely. Such views shall be taken into consideration on matters which concern them in accordance with their age and maturity.

2. In all actions relating to children, whether taken by public authorities or private institutions, the child's best interests must be a primary consideration.
3. Every child shall have the right to maintain on a regular basis a personal relationship and direct contact with both his or her parents, unless that is contrary to his or her interests.

Article 25
The rights of the elderly

The Union recognises and respects the rights of the elderly to lead a life of dignity and independence and to participate in social and cultural life.

Article 26
Integration of persons with disabilities

The Union recognises and respects the right of persons with disabilities to benefit from measures designed to ensure their independence, social and occupational integration and participation in the life of the community.

Chapter IV
SOLIDARITY

Article 27
Workers' right to information and consultation within the undertaking

Workers or their representatives must, at the appropriate levels, be guaranteed information and consul- tation in good time in the cases and under the conditions provided for by Community law and national laws and practices.

Article 28
Right of collective bargaining and action

Workers and employers, or their respective organisations, have, in accordance with Community law and national laws and practices, the right to negotiate and conclude collective agreements at the appropriate levels and, in cases of conflicts of interest, to take collective action to defend their interests, including strike action.

Article 29
Right of access to placement services

Everyone has the right of access to a free placement service.

Article 30
Protection in the event of unjustified dismissal

Every worker has the right to protection against unjustified dismissal, in accordance with Community law and national laws and practices.

Article 31
Fair and just working conditions

1. Every worker has the right to working conditions which respect his or her health, safety and dignity.
2. Every worker has the right to limitation of maximum working hours, to daily and weekly rest periods and to an annual period of paid leave.

Article 32
Prohibition of child labour and protection of young people at work

1. The employment of children is prohibited. The minimum age of admission to employment may not be lower than the minimum school-leaving age, without prejudice to such rules as may be more favourable to young people and except for limited derogations.
2. Young people admitted to work must have working conditions appropriate to their age and be protected against economic exploitation and any work likely to harm their safety, health or physical, mental, moral or social development or to interfere with their education.

Article 33
Family and professional life

1. The family shall enjoy legal, economic and social protection.
2. To reconcile family and professional life, everyone shall have the right to protection from dismissal for a reason connected with maternity and the right to paid maternity leave and to parental leave following the birth or adoption of a child.

Article 34
Social security and social assistance

1. The Union recognises and respects the entitlement to social security benefits and social services providing protection in cases such as maternity, illness, industrial accidents, dependency or old age, and in the

case of loss of employment, in accordance with the rules laid down by Community law and national laws and practices.

2. Everyone residing and moving legally within the European Union is entitled to social security benefits and social advantages in accordance with Community law and national laws and practices.

3. In order to combat social exclusion and poverty, the Union recognises and respects the right to social and housing assistance so as to ensure a decent existence for all those who lack sufficient resources, in accordance with the rules laid down by Community law and national laws and practices.

Article 35
Health care

Everyone has the right of access to preventive health care and the right to benefit from medical treatment under the conditions established by national laws and practices. A high level of human health protection shall be ensured in the definition and implementation of all Union policies and activities.

Article 36
Access to services of general economic interest

The Union recognises and respects access to services of general economic interest as provided for in national laws and practices, in accordance with the Treaty establishing the European Community, in order to promote the social and territorial cohesion of the Union.

Article 37
Environmental protection

A high level of environmental protection and the improvement of the quality of the environment must be integrated into the policies of the Union and ensured in accordance with the principle of sustainable development.

Article 38
Consumer protection

Union policies shall ensure a high level of consumer protection.

Chapter V
CITIZENS' RIGHTS

Article 39
Right to vote and to stand as a candidate at elections to the European Parliament

1. Every citizen of the Union has the right to vote and to stand as a candidate at elections to the European Parliament in the Member State in which he or she resides, under the same conditions as nationals of that State.
2. Members of the European Parliament shall be elected by direct universal suffrage in a free and secret ballot.

Article 40
Right to vote and to stand as a candidate at municipal elections

Every citizen of the Union has the right to vote and to stand as a candidate at municipal elections in the Member State in which he or she resides under the same conditions as nationals of that State.

Article 41
Right to good administration

1. Every person has the right to have his or her affairs handled impartially, fairly and within a reasonable time by the institutions and bodies of the Union.
2. This right includes:
   - the right of every person to be heard, before any individual measure which would affect him or her adversely is taken;
   - the right of every person to have access to his or her file, while respecting the legitimate interests of confidentiality and of professional and business secrecy;
   - the obligation of the administration to give reasons for its decisions.
3. Every person has the right to have the Community make good any damage caused by its insti- tutions or by its servants in the performance of their duties, in accordance with the general principles common to the laws of the Member States.
4. Every person may write to the institutions of the Union in one of the languages of the Treaties and must have an answer in the same language.

Article 42
Right of access to documents

Any citizen of the Union, and any natural or legal person residing or having its registered office in a Member State, has a right of access to European Parliament, Council and Commission documents.

Article 43
Ombudsman

Any citizen of the Union and any natural or legal person residing or having its registered office in a Member State has the right to refer to the Ombudsman of the Union cases of maladministration in the activities of the Community institutions or bodies, with the exception of the Court of Justice and the Court of First Instance acting in their judicial role.

Article 44
Right to petition

Any citizen of the Union and any natural or legal person residing or having its registered office in a Member State has the right to petition the European Parliament.

Article 45
Freedom of movement and of residence

1. Every citizen of the Union has the right to move and reside freely within the territory of the Member States.
2. Freedom of movement and residence may be granted, in accordance with the Treaty establishing the European Community, to nationals of third countries legally resident in the territory of a Member State.

Article 46
Diplomatic and consular protection

Every citizen of the Union shall, in the territory of a third country in which the Member State of which he or she is a national is not represented, be entitled to protection by the diplomatic or consular authorities of any Member State, on the same conditions as the nationals of that Member State.

Chapter VI
JUSTICE

Article 47
Right to an effective remedy and to a fair trial

1. Everyone whose rights and freedoms guaranteed by the law of the Union are violated has the right to an effective remedy before a tribunal in compliance with the conditions laid down in this Article.
2. Everyone is entitled to a fair and public hearing within a reasonable time by an independent and impartial tribunal previously established by law. Everyone shall have the possibility of being advised, defended and represented.
3. Legal aid shall be made available to those who lack sufficient resources in so far as such aid is necessary to ensure effective access to justice.

Article 48
Presumption of innocence and right of defence

1. Everyone who has been charged shall be presumed innocent until proved guilty according to law.
2. Respect for the rights of the defence of anyone who has been charged shall be guaranteed.

Article 49
Principles of legality and proportionality
of criminal offences and penalties

1. No one shall be held guilty of any criminal offence on account of any act or omission which did not constitute a criminal offence under national law or international law at the time when it was committed. Nor shall a heavier penalty be imposed than that which was applicable at the time the criminal offence was committed. If, subsequent to the commission of a criminal offence, the law provides for a lighter penalty, that penalty shall be applicable.
2. This Article shall not prejudice the trial and punishment of any person for any act or omission which, at the time when it was committed, was criminal according to the general principles recognised by the community of nations.
3. The severity of penalties must not be disproportionate to the criminal offence.

Article 50
Right not to be tried or punished twice in criminal proceedings for the same criminal offence

No one shall be liable to be tried or punished again in criminal proceedings for an offence for which he or she has already been finally acquitted or convicted within the Union in accordance with the law.

Chapter VII
GENERAL PROVISIONS

Article 51
Scope

1. The provisions of this Charter are addressed to the institutions and bodies of the Union with due regard for the principle of subsidiarity and to the Member States only when they are implementing Union law. They shall therefore respect the rights, observe the principles and promote the application thereof in accordance with their respective powers.
2. This Charter does not establish any new power or task for the Community or the Union, or modify powers and tasks defined by the Treaties.

Article 52
Scope of guaranteed rights

1. Any limitation on the exercise of the rights and freedoms recognised by this Charter must be provided for by law and respect the essence of those rights and freedoms. Subject to the principle of proportionality, limitations may be made only if they are necessary and genuinely meet objectives of general interest recognised by the Union or the need to protect the rights and freedoms of others.
2. Rights recognised by this Charter which are based on the Community Treaties or the Treaty on European Union shall be exercised under the conditions and within the limits defined by those Treaties.
3. In so far as this Charter contains rights which correspond to rights guaranteed by the Convention for the Protection of Human Rights and Fundamental Freedoms, the meaning and scope of those rights shall be the same as those laid down by the said Convention. This provision shall not prevent Union law providing more extensive protection.

Article 53
Level of protection

Nothing in this Charter shall be interpreted as restricting or adversely affecting human rights and fundamental freedoms as recognised, in their respective fields of application, by Union law and inter- national law and by international agreements to which the Union, the Community or all the Member States are party, including the European Convention for the Protection of Human Rights and Funda- mental Freedoms, and by the Member States' constitutions.

Article 54
Prohibition of abuse of rights

Nothing in this Charter shall be interpreted as implying any right to engage in any activity or to perform any act aimed at the destruction of any of the rights and freedoms recognised in this Charter or at their limitation to a greater extent than is provided for herein.

Social Democracy

Radicalise,
or it's over ...

Paul Mason

This is the full text of writer Paul Mason's planned address to the Europe Together conference in Brussels on 18 October 2017. In raising a 'new concept' of citizenship in Europe, it reaches into some of the deeper issues at stake as the UK government flounders in its attempt to leave the European Union.

◄ *Paul Mason in Brussels*

Lloyd Blankfein, CEO of Goldman Sachs, recently tweeted this:

> 'At IMF in DC. Puzzling that politics everywhere are so difficult when world's economies are (mostly) good and the world is (mostly) at peace.'

Here's my answer to the puzzle: neoliberalism is broken. By neoliberalism I do not mean simply the ideas of Hayek and Freidman – their ideology never described the actual system created by Thatcher, Reagan, Yeltsin and Deng Xiao Ping. By the word 'neoliberalism' I mean the whole global economic system of the world which drove growth and technological progress between 1989 and 2008 – but has now stopped.

For me, neoliberalism describes the system in its totality: the countries which borrow, import and consume; and the countries that save, lend, export and produce. When it worked, it drove a gross global imbalance. The logic of the imbalance was to create financial catastrophe.

As the economists Brender and Pisani wrote in 2010 – the only thing that could have rebalanced the world was the devastating financial crisis of 2008. So, since 2008, neoliberalism has been on life support: $15 trillion dollars worth of quantitative easing. You can keep an economy on life support for a long time. But you cannot keep an ideology on life support. The human brain demands coherence.

For many people in developed countries there is no coherent story of how their lives get better; they know their kids will be poorer than them; and they see an elite – like Mr Blankfein – that just doesn't get it. In fact, seeing the elite get richer and go on failing to get it is even more painful that simply staying poor.

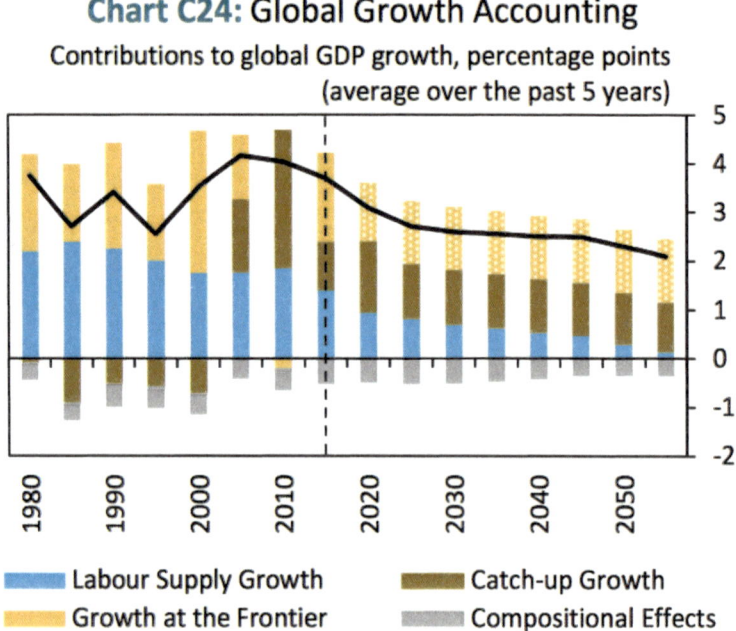

Chart C24: Global Growth Accounting
Contributions to global GDP growth, percentage points
(average over the past 5 years)

Legend:
- Labour Supply Growth
- Catch-up Growth
- Growth at the Frontier
- Compositional Effects
- Global GDP Growth

Consider this Bank of England analysis of the sources of global growth, past and future, produced in 2015.

The black line is growth – actual and projected. The coloured bars show what contributed to that growth. The chart shows that between 1975 and 2015 – the whole course of neoliberal globalisation – growth remained static, but what drove it changed. In the upswing of neoliberalism, before 2000, much of the growth comes from an expanding workforce – the so-called 'Great Doubling' – shown in blue; but there's also growth at the frontiers of productivity shown in yellow: that is better education, technological change.

After 2000, much of the growth is 'catch-up growth' as China and other BRICS countries [Brazil, Russia, India, South Africa] truly enter the world market. But look at the black line for the future. If the Bank's economists are right, there'll be less growth in the future than in the past 40 years. Most of it will be catch-up growth. None of it will be driven by technological change.

Though 99.9% of voters in Britain, France, Germany, Austria and the USA have never seen this graph, their behaviour and their psychology are beginning to reflect the suspicion that it is right: that the best days of capitalism are over. The shock is all the greater because neoliberalism was supposed to last forever. Like this forever, only better. Since 2008, neoliberalism's promise has been: like this forever, only worse.

In 2015 in my book *Postcapitalism*, I said we face a choice – ditch neoliberalism or it will destroy globalisation. That is what's happening. It's not just that we have xenophobic movements, violent misogyny and racism: we have sections of the business elite prepared to use these movements and sentiments to gain political power. Trump, the AfD in Germany, Le Pen in France, UKIP in the UK, the FPÖ in Austria all exhibit the essential characteristic Hannah Arendt described in her book on totalitarianism: they are an alliance of the 'elite and the mob'. Though they are in the main not classically fascist parties, they are succeeding because of two factors that the German sociologist Erich Fromm observed in the 1930s:

● Tiredness, combined with loneliness
● The exhaustion and failure of the left.

What the far right and the conservative parties are now converging around is not a return to the national state-led capitalism of the Keynesian era. If you listen to Trump, and to the right-wing British MP Jacob Rees-Mogg, and to the AfD in Germany, the project is national neoliberalism. It will not work. As the historian Charles Kindleberger reminds us, in his account of the Great Depression of the 1930s, when states enthusiastically compete negative sum games, the outcome is a smaller global economy.

What can we do? First we need to say clearly: neoliberalism is over. If social democracy's strategy was to generate a surplus through highly financial, globalised free-market economy, and distribute it downwards as a compensation for stagnant wages and atomised communities – that is no longer possible. The more you try to do it, the more you have to coerce competitive behaviour into people's lives: from the counter of the coffee bar, to the welfare system, to housing, to the process of finding someone to go on a date.

Promise number one of a radical social democracy should be: we will switch off the great privatisation machine.

Promise number two also costs you nothing: we will stop imposing, nudging and coersing market behaviour into people's lives – and foster, instead, human, collaborative impulses that 30 years of neoliberalism

suppressed. To do that we need the following:
- an alternative economic model
- a narrative of hope
- a social movement to fight for it
- party structures that can enable this to work, rather than hinder it.

This picture shows Jeremy Corbyn at the moment people spontaneously turned his name into a football song. In June 2017, we got 12 million people to vote for us because we offered the first two things: a clear policy alternative to neoliberalism and a narrative of hope.

I opposed the Third Way strategy in the 1990s, but I do recognise the Blair/Brown government delivered real advances in social justice. The Third Way strategy was logical if you believed neoliberalism would last forever. The problem we faced after 2010 was what to do now that neoliberalism was broken?

For five years, under Ed Miliband, we tried to avoid the problem. But in the meantime the tribal alliance that formed British social democracy was being pulled apart: by progressive nationalism in Scotland; by the xenophobia of UKIP in England and parts of Wales, which garnered four million votes in the European elections of 2014. But also by the emergence of a socially liberal and networked 'salariat' that was switched off from technocratic politics; which prioritised climate change, personal freedom, and so on.

Once we got to 2016, many working class people felt totally alienated from our political language, and viscerally worried about the impact of

European migration on public services. When the entire centre of politics, backed up by the liberal 'salariat', told them they could only reduce migration by leaving the European Union, 17 million decided to leave EU.

Even before Brexit it was obvious that only one thing could pull the alliance back together: economic radicalism and a vision of a new kind of capitalism beyond neoliberalism. That's why, when Jeremy Corbyn stood for the Labour leadership in 2015, tens of thousands of people joined the Party to vote for him. That's why in 2016, when the Party hierarchy, the majority of MPs and the UK media tried to depose him, more than 100,000 people joined in 48 hours to defend him. The road from winning the Party to destroying Theresa May's parliamentary majority was not easy.

Corbyn made mistakes. His team was inexperienced and was sometimes made to look incompetent by their enemies. In the Brexit referendum Corbyn tried to lead a Labour-only campaign, based on criticism and reform of Lisbon. The message was too complicated and got lost – above all because his answer to concerns on migration was long-term reform of the labour market, while our voters were being offered an easier short-term solution: leave.

In June 2017, twelve million people intervened into our internal argument and told us they liked the idea of a radical social democratic government and a soft Brexit. Two moments changed things.

First was the Manifesto. The moment it was leaked, the crowds around Corbyn started to be real, chaotic and spontaneous. By setting a strict fiscal rule – borrow only to invest – Labour gave itself the ability to promise two things: a 250 billion investment programme and a 50 billion programme of new taxes to reverse austerity.

In more than one UKIP stronghold I was told by Labour campaigners that active, politicised UKIP members came out of their houses and demanded Labour posters: 'the manifesto was all we needed,' they said. They just needed Labour to say it was going to start serving their communities, not the rich.

Second, we developed a narrative beyond politics. To hike your share of the youth vote to 64% in a single leap you need more than policies – you need a narrative. And in the final week of the election campaign, on the advice of our friends from Podemos, we consciously staged '*la remontada*'. We campaigned in defiance of our own image, almost 'against' our previous selves – seizing the high ground on issues of policing, national security and terror, which the right-wing press assumed were always negative for us.

Third, we developed an organisational form that matched the fast-moving online civil society of the electorate. Remember – Corbyn did not fully control the national executive or the Party HQ. So we used Momentum, a pro-Corbyn pressure group, to do what the party HQ did not: campaign in offensive parliamentary seats and not just ones we were trying to defend. We sent people to constituencies where in some cases local officials tried to turn them away, as they were deemed 'unwinnable', and we won them. We produced, at the cost of a few hundred pounds, satirical videos no official party would have ever sanctioned. One of them – in which a girl questions her conservative-voting father – was seen by eight million people.

We didn't win. We need to go further in creating a social movement, to gain – as Antonio Gramsci said – cultural hegemony in the wider society.

Also, let's be frank: what happened in Britain was possible because the political forces that would be in European United Left-Nordic Green Left (GUE-NGL) here in the European Parliament were already inside Labour. In Portugal a similar effect has been achieved through coalition. Elsewhere that may not be possible.

But we learned enough to offer some general advice. First, be radical. We must first offer a clear, plausible economic alternative to neoliberalism. End austerity. Regulate the labour market to promote the interests of workers. Build new homes for young people on a massive scale. Use state intervention to promote an innovative, high wage private sector. Preserve, modernise and extend the welfare state.

Beyond this, we must come up with concrete answers to the challenge of automation and precarious work. The citizens' basic income may be hard to implement at scale – but we should begin to explore it as a solution. Labour has committed to that. Equally effective can be the state provision of basic goods and services, cheap or free. 21st century social democracy cannot be – as André Gorz described Marxism – a utopia based on work.

In a world where many people lack power, lack confidence, and experience atomisation, small-scale collaborative projects – the credit union, the community garden, the workers' co-operative, the food bank – assume much greater importance. As with the socialism of Ferdinand Lassale, in Germany in the 1860s, such projects allow people to achieve things today that provide a link to what will be done tomorrow. Labour, for example, has pledged to double the size of the co-operative sector.

As for globalisation, to save it we must do less of it. End the tyranny of trade deals over social justice.

If neoliberalism is broken, social democracy cannot accept the Lisbon Treaty as the final form of the European Union. Today, if Corbyn is prepared to offer state aid, nationalisation, new progressive limits on the exploitation of migrant labour, it is because for the Labour Party the Lisbon Treaty never fully implanted itself inside our heads: outside the Euro, and effectively beyond the stability and growth pact – and, of course, as a big country – we have always been able to start from what's needed, second, how to achieve it within the Lisbon framework.

I think Juncker's White Paper allows social democratic parties an opportunity: to formulate a sixth option – a Europe of social justice, where low wage zones and social dumping are forbidden. If some countries do not want to be in that Europe, they can travel at a slower pace. Either way, the key is to switch off the Lisbon Treaty that is inside your head.

Probably the biggest challenge will be migration and asylum. The Austrian election result is the latest example: people in relatively prosperous countries are witholding consent because, though some are simply xenophobes and racists, many others cannot see the social justice in sharing scarce resources with people who arrive randomly and suddenly.

The answer is not to close the borders of Europe. We need inward migration to Europe and the maximum amount of freedom of movement compatible with retaining consent for migration. The answer is to win back consent for migration by taking control of it, to manage the domestic labour market actively, and to administer asylum justice fairly. And to equalise minimum wages and social benefits upwards across Europe.

Above all, I urge you to fight for a new concept of citizenship in Europe. In Britain the main hostility was, first, to East European migration. In the EU27 it is probably resistance to the arrival of asylum seekers from outside. But in both cases, it is hard to defend migration using the concept of citizenship the EU has adopted – whereby your citizenship is primarily economic.

From the British experience I believe it was not primarily the low wage effect of inward migration that drove hostility to free movement; it was the arrival of three million extra people entitled to use taxpayer-funded services in a period of austerity. The fact that many of them worked in the NHS and public services was not enough to convince some people that the overall impact was beneficial.

Many people were instinctively hostile to the European Union's abstract notion of citizenship, which says the social capital, traditions and community values of existing residents do not count – and citizenship resides only in your ability to travel and work. At its most existential level, our problem is that we have allowed the constitution of Europe to be framed around an economic system that no longer works. Neoliberalism, writes the British economist William Davies, is the disenchantment of politics by economics.

Right-wing populism is the re-enchantment of politics by nationalism, racism, nostalgia and misogyny.

Radical social democracy must be the re-enchantment of politics by social justice and through a concept of citizenship based on the whole human being – the *zöon politikon*, not *homo economicus*.

Jettisoning nuclear dogma

Commander
Robert Green
Royal Navy (Ret'd)

The landmark Treaty on the Prohibition of Nuclear Weapons was agreed at the United Nations in New York in July 2017, and now gathers signatures. Meanwhile, the International Campaign for the Abolition of Nuclear Weapons (ICAN) deservedly receives the 2017 Nobel Peace Prize in recognition of its long-term efforts to advance the Treaty. Cdr Robert Green and Kate Dewes have performed unstinting work in pursuit of this Treaty through the Aotearoa/New Zealand Peace Foundation. Whilst in New York for the historic deliberations at the UN, Cdr Green recounted his own nuclear biography and drew some pertinent wider lessons.

◄ *Cdr Green's influential book*

As a former operator of British nuclear weapons, next year will mark a significant anniversary for me: it will be fifty years since my indoctrination into the dogma of nuclear deterrence.

In 1968, I was a 24-year-old Lieutenant bombardier-navigator in Buccaneer strike jets deployed aboard a Royal Navy aircraft-carrier, when my pilot and I were told we had been chosen as a nuclear crew. The process of being given a top secret security clearance was followed by indoctrination regarding the huge responsibility of this honour, and details of the 10-kiloton WE177 freefall bomb we would use. We then had to plan how to attack our assigned target: a Soviet military air base on the outskirts of Leningrad.

Thirty years later, as I landed at St Petersburg airport for an anti-nuclear conference, I was shocked to realise it had been my target. When I told our Russian hosts, they put me on local TV with an interpreter. I apologised for having obeyed orders, which would have resulted in massive civilian casualties and collateral damage to their ancient capital. Then I told them I had learned that nuclear weapons would not save me, or them.

My breakout from pro-nuclear brainwashing was slow and gradual, inhibited by tribal loyalty, peer pressure, initial unquestioning trust in my leaders, and deference to their mindset, linked to ambition to succeed in my chosen career. Breakout began in 1972 after I switched from navigating nuclear strike jets to anti-submarine helicopters. Because our lightweight torpedoes were too slow to catch Soviet nuclear submarines, we were given a nuclear depth-bomb. The problem was that, unlike a strike jet, our helicopter was too slow to escape the detonation; so this would be a suicide mission. When I complained, my leaders assured me we probably would never have to use it; besides, I didn't want to cut short a glittering career, did I? So I fell silent; but the first doubts set in.

In 1979, I was a newly promoted Commander in the Ministry of Defence in London, looking after an Admiral whose responsibilities included recommending how best to replace the UK Polaris nuclear-armed submarine force. Mrs Thatcher had just come to power; and she wanted Trident. I watched as the Naval Staff warned that this would exceed the Polaris system's capability, and its huge cost would mean cuts in useful warships.

Thatcher drove the Trident decision through. Then, sure enough, in 1981, the government announced a major defence review in order to pay for Trident. With my prospects of further promotion receding, on top of concern that I couldn't justify Trident, I applied for redundancy.

My application was approved one week into the 1982 Falklands War. I had to stay until after we won, and I had handed over my job as Staff Intelligence Officer to the Commander in Chief Fleet, who ran the war from the command bunker on the outskirts of London. I was in charge of the 40-strong team providing round the clock intelligence support to the one Polaris submarine on so-called deterrent patrol, as well as the rest of the Fleet.

The Falklands War was a close-run thing. The French had sold the Argentine Navy sea-skimming Exocet missiles, which we had no answer to for a while; several of our ships were sunk, and colleagues killed. If one of our aircraft carriers or troopships had been taken out, we could have risked defeat. What would Thatcher have done? Before the war she had been the most unpopular British Prime Minister in history; now her political career was on the line – and she had nuclear weapons.

After leaving the Navy, I heard rumours of an extremely secret contingency plan – understandably not shared with the Navy – to move the patrolling Polaris submarine south within range of Buenos Aires. It wasn't needed; however, in 2006 it was revealed that Thatcher had phoned French President Mitterrand after the first British ships were sunk, threatening to nuke Argentina if he didn't give her the secret frequency of the Exocet guidance system to jam it. Convinced that she was serious, he did so; and soon after, we began to neutralise Exocet.

This raised for me the nightmare of a desperate British leader having the option of using nuclear weapons, and the ignominy of our submariners being ordered to commit such a war crime. British possession of nuclear weapons had not deterred Argentine President General Galtieri from invading. Had Thatcher threatened to use nuclear weapons, probably Galtieri would have called her bluff very publicly, and relished watching US President Reagan try to rein her in. If he had failed, a nuclear strike would have compounded the ignominy of defeat, the British case for retaining the Falkland Islands lost in international outrage over such a war crime.

Seven years later, my justification for supporting nuclear deterrence collapsed with the Berlin Wall, and subsequent dismantling of the Warsaw Pact. However, it took Iraq's invasion of Kuwait in 1990 to make me speak out. When President Bush senior doubled the number of ground troops to evict Iraq, my intelligence training warned me that this would be a punitive expedition. If Saddam Hussein was personally threatened, he could attack Israel with Scud missiles, possibly with chemical warheads, in order to split the US-led coalition and become the Arabs' champion. If a chemical-headed Scud attack caused heavy casualties, Israel's leader Shamir would come under massive pressure to respond with a nuclear strike on Baghdad. The Arab nations would erupt in fury, Israel's security would be destroyed forever, and Russia would be sucked in.

In January 1991, I joined the growing British anti-war movement by speaking to a crowd of 20,000 in Trafalgar Square – not the best move or place for an ex-Commander. A week later, following the launch of the allied blitzkrieg, the first Iraqi Scud attack hit Tel Aviv. For the first time, the second city of a *de facto* nuclear weapon state had been attacked and its capital threatened. Worse still for nuclear deterrence, the attacker did not have nuclear weapons. Israelis, cowering in gas masks in basements, learned that their nuclear deterrent had failed. 38 more Scud attacks followed, fortunately with no chemical warheads and miraculously causing few casualties. Bush rushed to offer Shamir Patriot missiles and other military aid, and congratulated Israel on its restraint.

Interestingly, in both this case and the one I described in the Falklands War, nuclear weapon possession had been used to coerce a fellow nuclear-armed state.

Meanwhile, in London the Irish Republican Army just missed wiping out the entire British War Cabinet meeting in 10 Downing Street with a mortar bomb launched through the roof of a van. A more direct threat to the government could barely be imagined; and Polaris was exposed as an impotent irrelevance.

Belatedly forced to research the history of nuclear weapons, I learned that the UK bore considerable responsibility for initiating and spreading the nuclear arms race. Having joined in the Manhattan project, Britain became the first medium-sized power with delusions of grandeur to threaten nuclear terrorism. Here in the United States, in denial over its atrocities in Hiroshima and Nagasaki, the mantra of nuclear deterrence was used to play on people's fears, and justify sustaining the unaccountable, highly profitable scientific and military monster bequeathed by the Manhattan project. Successive British governments, desperate to keep their seat at the top table of world powers, seized upon this confidence trick, endlessly repeating its bogus claims – uncritically propagated by experts and mainstream media – to the point that it echoed the fable of the emperor with no clothes.

Feeling much like the child who pointed this out – as I described in my 2010 book *Security Without Nuclear Deterrence* (which Spokesman will republish in 2018) – my experience taught me that nuclear deterrence, far from providing security, promotes insecurity through stimulating hostility, mistrust, nuclear arms racing and proliferation. What is more, because of these realities and its insoluble credibility problem, it is highly vulnerable to failure. As for extended nuclear deterrence, far from providing a so-called 'nuclear umbrella' to non-nuclear US allied states, it acts as a 'lightning rod' attracting insecurity to them, because any use of nuclear weapons by the US on their behalf would inevitably escalate to all-out nuclear war. The truth is that the US uses extended deterrence to control its allies for its own purposes. Prime Minister David Lange, who led New Zealand's breakout thirty years ago, correctly called it 'fool's gold'.

Similarly, the US uses its nuclear sharing arrangement with certain European states to sustain subservience to NATO, and block progress to a nuclear weapon-free world.

Let me close by honouring two controversial, courageous US Generals – both called Butler. Like me, they broke free from acceptance of their government's and peer group's mindset and indoctrination. On retirement in 1935, US Marine General Smedley Butler wrote a searing critique of his military experience, entitled *War is a Racket*.

Seventy years later, US Air Force General Lee Butler, after running the entire US strategic nuclear war machine, came out against nuclear deterrence. In 2016, he published his memoirs entitled *Uncommon Cause*, in Volume II of which he recounts the powerful, poignant story of his breakout. I must speak bluntly: stripped of jargon, what he confirms in effect is that nuclear deterrence is a vast protection racket by a US-led organised crime syndicate, who use it as a counterfeit currency of power, and whose principal beneficiary is the military-industrial complex. His findings should be required reading for the syndicate members, for all those who have fallen victim to their scam, and those of us who are leading the struggle to face them down and bring them to justice.

This is why the Treaty on the Prohibition of Nuclear Weapons, now open for signature, prohibits threat of use, and includes language explaining what that means. It is not enough to assume that use encompasses threat. The fact that the currently deployed UK Trident submarine is described as on 'deterrent patrol', despite being at days' notice to fire with no assigned target, confirms this need.

Robert Green (right) and Tony Simpson outside Bertrand Russell's flat in Bury Place, London. At the other end of the street, a new plaque commemorates Joseph Rotblat and the Pugwash Conferences on Science and World Affairs, which he and Russell established.

NATO's nuclear 'sleight-of-hand'

Paul H Johnstone

For two Cold War decades, Dr Johnstone worked in the 'upper echelons' of US intelligence, including during the extended Berlin Crisis of 1961 which saw the construction of the Wall dividing the city. Discussing a draft memo on 'NATO military policy in the Berlin Crisis', he probed the 'judgment' that 'the West had a preponderant advantage both in nuclear striking power and in capacity to survive a surprise [Soviet] attack'. This excerpt is from his posthumous memoir, From MAD to Madness: Inside Pentagon Nuclear War Planning *(Clarity Press, Atlanta, 2017), which is published with a commentary by his daughter, Diana Johnstone.*

… The Soviets could deliver comparatively few weapons on North America in any case, and in the best case Western superiority would be overwhelming. Soviet counter-damage would be 'severe, but not so serious as to endanger (US) national survival'. However, the Soviets probably could seriously damage NATO Europe even after a full-scale pre-emptive attack, and to this extent their claim that NATO Europe was their hostage was valid.

On the other side, the acknowledged Soviet preponderance of conventional strength made it impossible for the Allies to oppose Soviet aggressions successfully by conventional means, and local and conventional military opposition to the Soviets could successfully serve but one purpose, which was to confront the Soviets with the clear choice between ceasing aggression and nuclear war. But even tactical nuclear weapons may trigger general nuclear war at low levels of engagement, and so therefore, 'It might be advisable to strike first strategically rather than engage in large scale tactical nuclear war'. Attaining goals without nuclear war remained as the NATO objective, but the Soviets should be regularly reminded of Western nuclear superiority and of 'Western readiness to engage in general war for our vital interests…' But because public emphasis on the fact that 'as action policy, the West will make every effort to strike first when the general situation demands general war' was destabilising, the 'declaratory policy', in contrast, 'would focus on our nuclear superiority, our ability to survive a Soviet first strike with dominant nuclear forces intact, and our readiness to fight nuclear war in defence of our vital interests'. Here was a sort of ambiguity that left little doubt of what was left unsaid.

This draft was given the unqualified blessing of the Joint Chiefs of Staff by a formal memo on November 15, which described it as a 'well developed, forthright summation of US assessment, concepts and policies', and added that: 'It adequately reflects the basic concepts of US military policy with respect to Berlin and could serve as a basis for discussion with selected allies on occasion.'

Which it did, following approval by McNamara and Kennedy. Chancellor Konrad Adenauer, accompanied by his Defence Minister Franz Josef Strauss, spent four days in Washington from November 21 to 25, and in conversations with Kennedy recited the longstanding German scepticism over the effectiveness of the projected 30 conventional division NATO force, as well as over the preferred American tactic of gradually escalating military actions. Agreement was reached on enough of the issues to assure that the US and the Federal Republic of Germany could present a common front, especially in those areas where there might be negotiations with the Soviets. It is not explicit in the available records of the meetings that Kennedy actually used the International Security Affairs (ISA) [Defense Department] paper, although it seems probable he did, because Adenauer was sufficiently reassured to bring an end to the habitual German objections to our contingency planning proposals.

In follow-up actions just before the regular NATO December meetings, McNamara and Nitze made the contents known to the defence ministers of Britain and France, and Strauss's deputy, in a somewhat theatrical manoeuvre. Getting these officials alone where there was no chance of note-taking or making a record, McNamara read the paper aloud to them, letting them look over his shoulder as he read, then quickly withdrawing it. Such was the sleight-of-hand. Other NATO nations were, for the time being, left in the dark.

By this time – early December – the 1961 phase of the Berlin crisis was receding, and everyone knew it, although there were few who did not fear it would erupt again at any time. And it did, in February-March of 1962, as a test of our nerves over air corridor access. We were becoming much less jumpy about it by then, because we were learning from experience that the Soviets were just playing their game of seeking, by every conceivable annoyance or threat they believed would not provoke us into drastic reaction, to extort concessions they had no legal or moral right to ask, but which we found it difficult to deny because of our highly vulnerable, exposed position in Berlin.

There continued to be nasty little hold-ups on the Autobahn and on the railroads into Berlin, many minor tragedies along the Wall and in the no man's land separating West from East Berlin. The minimum Soviet objectives of solidifying their control of East Germany and East Berlin had been largely assured, if not fully accomplished and formally acknowledged. It is not clear how much more, or how much less, they could have gained, had our policies and actions varied within the compass of what was responsibly considered. It is a reasonable speculation that had we been either more aggressively defiant of Soviet moves, or readier to concede their demands, that a vastly different resolution of the issues would have occurred. The rapidly spreading unrest in East Germany in the period before the Wall was highly explosive, and that situation, combined with the generations-old Russian fear of invasion, especially by a militaristic Germany, might very easily have led the Kremlin into risks it would not have undertaken under any circumstances considered less threatening. We might therefore have precipitated the general war everyone dreaded by taking steps that prevented stabilisation of East Germany. On the other hand, had we seemed less resolute, the Soviets might well have sought to extend their grip on Germany by measures that would have ignited the German hatred of the Russians and precipitated violence that could quickly have become uncontrollable, and in this way have led to general war. Obviously, this is conjecture. But it can hardly be called mere conjecture that people on both sides who had the power to initiate nuclear war were considering, in all seriousness, taking steps that, from all we know, would have led us into that general war. We were that close to it …

Inclusive European Security?

Russia and the EU in the Post-Western World

Veronika Sušová-Salminen[1]

We continue our discussion of the problems of NATO. The author is a Czech historian based in Finland.

There has been a lot of talk of a new Cold War between the West and Russia, even though the metaphor itself is not appropriate in today's globalised context. It is not a very fitting analytical description. Firstly, there is no clear ideological and systemic struggle between Russia and the West; this means that Russia does not offer any alternative system or ideology. It is acting through the same system – the capitalist one, with post-Soviet nuances and deformations.

Secondly, the confrontation between Russia and the West is strongly positioned in gaps in communication and shared virtual spaces. Here, the key feature is the battle between competing narratives, their intermingling deconstructions and mutual blame of propaganda, fake news and so on. This makes it extremely difficult to nurture a spirit of dialogue and objectivity.

The recent strife with Russia is a composite part of the next cyclical crisis of capitalism and cannot be viewed beyond systemic circumstances – in particular, the dynamics of the 2007-2009 crisis, or 'Great Recession', represent an important factor. Furthermore, it is important to remember the key principle involved in the organisation of foreign relations: an anarchy, intended to mean the non-existence of supreme authority over nation states, which are fundamental (although not the only) political actors. Despite talks of liberal order, this is its principal characteristic.

Thus, classical instruments and characteristics of an international conflict are in motion, as well as a new version of a security dilemma without a fixed point to indicate the beginning of its downward spiral. However, the results are clear: growth of insecurity (located along the EU-Russian border and in so-called new Eastern Europe), militarisation and, of course, an increase in military spending and an arms race.

In Western mainstream discourses, Russia is to be blamed alone for the failure of the European security architecture. As in the past, it is Russia's *otherness* that represents a key argument here.[2] Russia is pictured as being a non-democratic, non-EUropean and neo-imperial rogue state. It is also blamed for disintegration processes in the EU, for aggression against Ukraine, for breaking international law (interestingly, by those who were breaking it before, too) and for cyber interventions in political processes. All these problems are presented as Russian issues, not as failures in interaction and mutual relations within the international system characterised by a conflict of interests. In the EU, Russia is portrayed as an old-fashioned and outdated power with conservative or even neo-fascist ideology, contrary to Europe's liberal ideal.[3] Russia's ideological peculiarity is perceived as problematic.

NATO, a Cold War organisation, is back on track and the EU is trying to use Russia as a common enemy and antipode of European liberal prosperity and ideals. And so, nearly 30 years after the celebrated fall of the Berlin Wall, new walls are being built, some of them symbolic and some of them real.[4] It is difficult not to view this as a failure and as the modern version of the old European story: a new division in Europe that echoes European imperial history and the warmongering discourses of both sides, using more or less sophisticated images of the enemy as a consolidating instrument.

Ukraine as a catalyst

The Ukrainian crisis represents an important part of this story, but it is not the only source of recent alienation/confrontation between the West (the EU and USA) and Russia. The 2014 crisis became a catalyst of already existing problems that are both internal and external in their nature. In Ukraine, it was a never-ending story of internal stagnation, corruption, state capture by competing oligarchic clans, lack of justice, underlying inequalities, lack of rule of law, and the need to channel the new wave of popular discontent via fresh 'revolution' led by old political faces with new pro-European slogans. In the end, EU neighbourhood policies were much tested in Ukraine and can hardly be evaluated as a success in terms of security and peace in Europe.

The Ukrainian crisis, as a European crisis, was an embodiment of ignorance in terms of geography and its role in the formation of foreign politics and security concerns. This is true not only for Kiev but also in the European metropolises that invited Ukraine into the club as an associated country (in fact, a new type of imperial euro-hierarchy: member state – candidate – associated country). It occurred even when a negative dynamic of two Eastern enlargements for the EU was evident in the context of the Great Recession/euro crisis. And the negative consequences for Ukraine and its relationship with Russia were inevitably imprinted on the internal and external dynamics of the EU.

Of course, it was flattering to see that the European Union still had its magnetism in the middle of deep structural crisis. But it was here, in Ukraine, where EU weakening soft power collided with the classical great power arsenal and *Realpolitik*. If Ukraine was caught in an identity-based conflict (West or Russia, both mutually exclusive), then the EU was trapped in the dynamics lying between two versions of Europe: new Atlanticism and neo-continentalism. The ideology of EUrope (and not Europe, as a diverse place where different experiences, cultures, political systems and histories intersect) contributed to the final blow.

Russian red line

The Russian reaction to this one-way ticket towards a new European Ukraine was based on geopolitical calculations. Ukraine's NATO membership and the map of Eastern Europe were to play for. Russia wanted a military neutral Ukraine, where her political influence would mean that NATO, defined in Moscow as a foreign policy instrument of the USA, would not expand further and weaken Russia's security position. Together with Ukraine, it was also a member of the newly created Eurasian Economic Union (EAEU), seen in Moscow as a composite part of pan-European common space. In the West, the EU, and in the East, the EAEU as complementary parts of wider Europe; this was the Russian proposition defined by Vladimir Putin in 2012. It was a continental and pluriversal approach to Europe (as a composite part of broader Eurasia), which however refused the idea of Europe as the European Union with its normative power arsenal or 'moral geopolitics' (Jószef Böröcz).[5] In fact, it was a post-Western vision which reflected the idea of multipolarity and which may be understood as a phenomenon of the post-Western world.

Moreover, Moscow tends to consider primarily security/geopolitical categories, taking into account geographical conditions and frameworks. Her *peripheral* position means that Moscow cannot rely on a strong soft power arsenal. So far, every former Soviet Bloc country that has joined the

EU has also been integrated into NATO. These occurrences, as recent history shows, have gone hand in hand. This is one of the reasons why relations between the European Union and Russia turned quite bitter from 2007 onwards.

NATO was one of the key generators of Cold War dynamics in Europe. It was a clear instrument of US predominance after 1945 and, more harshly, its parallel existence made the EU rather 'a civil wing' of NATO, as Richard Sakwa argues.[6] The processes of association/accession to the EU related to NATO membership also meant that NATO expanded geographically eastward.

On the map, the picture is simple: NATO moved closer to Russian borders, letting Russia out, but not offering any kind of diplomatic compromise. These processes left Russia on the margins of Europe, which expected it to either 'deal with it' or 'change' (to become democratic and liberal according to Western criteria) to even be considered for inclusion. The missionary approach which worked in Central East Europe failed in Russia with its great power identity. Badly.

Figure 1: The Baltic-Black sea axis, a key Russian security space, and NATO

Russia, whether Yeltsin's or Putin's, or 'pro-Western' or 'anti-Western', has always been critical of NATO enlargement. Euromaidan in Ukraine brought its potential membership of NATO back to the table, something which was a pronounced aim of many Ukrainian politicians in the past (see 2008 Bucharest NATO summit). After Euromaidan, it is a matter of chosen security and Ukraine's political future. From a geopolitical and security perspective, it represented a destabilising factor in the strategic space along the Baltic Sea and Black Sea axis – historically, a geopolitically crucial area for Russia in terms of cultural geopolitics and security. Thus, the potential of Ukrainian NATO membership is likely to be a source of confrontation and security concerns in Russia.

The European Union, its politicians, but also many academics were surprised by Russia's radical reaction. It took an unprecedented step, taking over Crimea with Russian naval bases on the peninsula and covert political/military intervention in eastern Ukraine. This created a new spot of frozen conflict in post-Soviet space. Suddenly, it was clear that the European Union's geopolitics of morality (or soft power) would not be effective here. Instead, it met with an old-fashioned resistance that combines *Realpolitik* and force with a rather new version of post-modern communication style.

Atlanticist EUrope

The old instruments of international politics were in motion, even when many believed that they were extinct thanks to the European Union. Of course, this was a shock. The tragedy of the EU, its strong defence and security dependency on NATO, and its main sponsor – the USA – was once again brought to the fore. In terms of soft power, the EU still succeeded in pro-reform Ukraine, but Russia was a completely different story. For peace and security on the European (and not EUropean) continent, it would be the next source of insecurity. At this point, it was clear that an *ideologically* based deal could not be made with Russia.

The Ukrainian crisis has shown little autonomous space for the European Union in its own continent. This limited independence may be strategically viewed as a key sign of the irrelevancy of the EU as a continental world power, typified by shifting global power (from the Atlantic towards Asia). And finally, this reduced autonomy, granted by security dependency on overseas USA, is asymmetric with potential as well as real impacts of the Ukrainian conflict – since it is situated in a shared continent, in the direct proximity of the European Union, creating an EU buffer zone that became territorially destabilised. On the other hand, the USA is overseas and outside Eurasian dynamics of power shifts and destabilisation centres, securing it from any critical impacts.

The key player – the USA – was set to limit Russian influence in the post-Soviet sphere and to react to Russian military modernisation, undertaken during Putin's third presidency. A consolidated and modernised army, and a new Eurasian regional platform with Russia as its leader was certainly not in US interests. As John Mearsheimer writes, the US strategy in different regions of the world is based on the following: do not allow the emergence of any regional hegemon.[7] With this logic, the regional hegemony of Russia in Northern Eurasia would certainly not be welcome in Washington. A strong strategic partnership based on plurality or pluriversality between the European Union and Russia would change the dynamics and balance of power in Eurasia.

The composite part of the US strategy is a full de-legitimisation of any kind of compromise with Russia. It usually depicts Russia as a country which is plotting the great war against Europe to resurrect its old empire. Russia as an independent player in world politics is made practically illegitimate: it has no legitimate concerns or interests. The struggle for legitimacy is a traditional part of international politics, and this is one of the latest examples. Under current circumstances, it works based on post-modern communication strategies where deconstruction meets new narratives and simulacra become 'facts'.

The compromise based on traditional diplomacy and negotiation is presented as immoral, while the factual unilateral dictate of the USA, with tragic consequences for global stability, is rather concealed. It is Western normativity which is used as a weapon: Russia is *other* and needs to change first before being spoken with. Russia must commit to Western values and transform itself in order to become a proper partner for the West. In fact, it means that Russia must abandon its position, humbly submit and change. There is little interest in having sources of Russian differences, such as the failure of transformation, neoliberal capitalism, and post-Soviet syndrome merging with it. For too many, *verstehen* (in the Weberian sense) [empathic understanding of human behaviour] has become the same as an apology. This attitude (which has its roots in imperial/colonial hegemony) is a source of Russian conservative stance – it is reactionary in one way, but emancipatory in another. It should not be forgotten that the denial of access to Europe has a deep consequence for Russian national as well as geocultural identity.

This missionary approach of the West is a hegemonic strategy of domination. The failures of transformation processes and weakened post-

Soviet statehood, mixed with cultural globalisation impacts, have caused Russia to turn to its roots once again (as in the 1880s and 1890s). It has begun its 'invention of traditions', such as Neo-Eurasianism and its newfound popularity, and the revival of Russian traditions in politics and popular culture. As before in history, Russia is currently positioning itself as an 'authentic' guardian of European traditions and values, appealing to conservativism in European societies.

Russia in American politics

We have also witnessed Russia become a key issue in US domestic politics[8] and a weapon to neutralise and de-legitimate any suggestions to change the post-Ukrainian confrontational style of politics towards Russia. In this regard, there are some echoes of the Cold War as a specific genre. Indeed, as a recent article in *Foreign Affairs* admits, the enemy image (of the Soviet Union and Soviet system) is much missed in today's USA as a strategy to keep domestic politics together.[9]

Furthermore, the Trump Administration formally finalised NATO's next enlargement in the Balkans: Montenegro was taken into the club, and there are signs that the next in line could be Macedonia. The lack of a radical shift in such politics has represented a main security irritant for Russia.

On the other hand, the Trump position towards US global hegemony is different and less convenient than many would expect. Trump plans to transform US foreign politics into openly egoistic policies without courting hypocrisy. Such hypocrisy often masked the USA's real intentions – meaning that it was universalising US interests as the interests of all humankind – but it also created certain limitations to the openly vulgar unilateralism.

Even so, President Trump is pushing NATO members to spend more money on 'defence' (2% GDP), despite being well aware that it is the US military-industrial complex which will cash in on the new investments. It is a new kick to the militarisation of Europe and the global arms race. This is a new form of neo-imperial tribute to be made in order to 'make America great again' at home. But it hardly means that with new obligations the power will be shared more equally on a decision-making level. Or, more precisely, that the US leadership under Trump will be more shared and based on dialogue and co-operation.

Thus, despite and due to the anti-Russian campaign against the US President at home, Trump has not challenged or changed any of the ongoing processes launched by the previous administration. So far, his administration continues with militarisation of the Eastern border in

Europe – by means of a higher military presence of the US army in the Baltic states, Poland and Romania, and NATO military exercises in Eastern Europe. In July 2017, there was a new military exercise in the Black Sea, which was unprecedented in form and content according to an official statement.[10] Trump's visit to Warsaw in July 2017 recently demonstrated that the road to détente is rather bumpy, unclear and very partial (limited to one deal about ceasefire in Syria). No doubt, the Russian side is reacting to these steps on the Western border (of Russia) in the same way, bringing about an accumulation effect and reproducing insecurity.

This is a typical example of a 'security dilemma', a spiral of actions and reactions that lead to increasing militarisation and arms racing.[11] More guns are presented as a security measure while the other side reacts in the same way. This means increasing tension and uncertainties in the European continent, which cannot be separated from the wider Eurasian land mass. Both sides will claim that the actions of the other side force them to respond 'adequately'.

If we look beyond Europe, we find the next potential hot spot of security competition and tensions. This is the situation on the Korean Peninsula where the USA continues to install a new THAAD anti-ballistic system. This military infrastructure is part of the US defence system, and was not welcomed by China or Russia, both countries in geographical proximity. Besides NATO enlargement there is a second major irritant to Russia: US withdrawal from the Anti-Ballistic Missile (ABM) Treaty. Russia interprets it in terms of 'strategic balance', including that of nuclear deterrent forces, and argues that imbalance will end in more global insecurity.

And, of course, another hot spot reflects Russian-US competition over Syria, or more broadly, the Near East gambit, which transferred this competition to the key region of Eurasia and of US geopolitical interest. Recently, there have been some signs of a possible partial co-operation in Syria, but we are still far from being able to say that one agreed ceasefire is a road to complex détente between the US and Russia. The new sanctions imposed against Russia mean that this will be not the case.

The Trump effect and the tragedy of EU-East

Trump and his new approach towards the international role of the United States, including egoistic pragmatism and demands, has been challenging for Brussels as well as other European capitals, particularly Berlin and Paris. Trump is also less enthusiastic about the European Union, which should not be forgotten. The Trump effect somewhat revived the idea of the European security system within the EU. But it is still questionable how much it is a serious and plausible process, and how much it is considered alongside Russia in a different role from that of the 'enemy'.

It is especially painful to observe the tragic role of Central East European states in the space between Germany and Russia over the course of the last 25 years. In short, their governments converted historical grievances into politics for the future, including those towards Russia. To escape their traumatic pasts (including the systemic *peripherality),* they failed to construct a co-operative mediation policy between the European Union and Russia. Historical grievances, fear or phobia, and Orientalist prejudices, within the ideologically defined 'return to Europe' (Europe intended as the European Union) became a key foreign political paradigm. Meanwhile, the region relies on the US and has repeatedly proved its loyalty by supporting the US government's most controversial steps, including the intervention in Iraq and Middle East destruction. This peripheral EUrope, culturally ambivalent ('Eastern margin of the West' – 'Western margin of the East' if we use such a meta-geographical dictionary) and insecure, came to be a source of liability, fear and uncompromising anti-Russian politics in the EU and NATO.

Instead of stepping in and learning from the past's harsh lessons, warning against confrontation with Russia, trying to build bridges and dialogue based on a strong knowledge of Russia, and searching for strategic balance, Central East Europe mostly supported and still supports one great power against another. To secure peace and its historical survival, it accepts the game of confrontation and militarisation. It seems it matters little that it is this region that becomes a main area of uncertainties and confrontation as a direct consequence of such politics. It is on the border of the Baltic states (Baltic Sea), Poland and in the Balkans (Black Sea) where tensions, military/spy incidents, and other forms of militarisation are, and will be, increasingly present. But these are countries which prefer to enforce anti-Russian militarization, and are involved in Orientalising Russia. They are compensating their own Orientalist (inferior) status in Europe, fixed during the accession process of 'Europeanisation', as a way to integrate into West European political institutions.

It also seems to be of little importance that there is a new fence being built between Russia in the East and EUrope in the border areas, in a way we recognise from the past. Those who were left – often involuntarily – behind the Iron Curtain are involved in moving it on their own borders. In fact, they are filling the buffer-zone role once again, if we apply the terminology of classical geopolitics.

Is the West ready for global coexistence?

There is a more general question. What does the future hold for the West and the European Union in our global but *diverse* world? Or to put it differently, what if Russian *otherness* is one of many in the increasingly post-Western world, which will be much more *hybrid* than normatively West-centric in the future? Are the West and the EU ready? Does military force provide the answer to weakening economic and cultural power?

The time of Western hegemony comes slowly but clearly to an end. Not only is the European core living under the long shadows of two imperialistic wars in 1914 and 1939; both were a composite part of *Finis Europae*, which meant that the gravity of the capitalist system was moved to the USA, on the Western shores of the Atlantic. Thus, Atlanticism is the product of this systemic history of Western capitalism – partly historically necessary and a bitter result of self-destruction of West European imperialism, and partly ideological. The still-existing security system of EUrope with NATO (and the USA) as its pillars was an unplanned consequence of Cold War competition between two superpowers.

In today's diverse but interconnected world, the soft power based on narcissist Eurocentrism is not and will not be enough. The war for weakening hegemony of the West (including the USA) is not the answer. Western normativity is meeting, and will meet more openly, different types of hybrids as a result of globalisation and colonialism. Western universalism (which is itself nothing less than a product of empire) will be ever more challenged culturally and politically as well as economically.[12]

Thus, relations with *other* Russia act as a litmus test for the European Union of the future. Russia questions the position of the EU in the European (not EUropean) continent, to which it is a significant and inevitable neighbour, in two different ways, at least.

The first is associated with soft power or cultural hegemony of the West and the European Union. What is Europe? This question has different answers – and Russia has its own answer, which is not necessarily wrong because it is *not the same* as that within the EU. The second set of problems relates to power asymmetries in terms of military capabilities and economy on the continent as well as in the rest of the world. Russia is still relatively strong in terms of military force, but more vulnerable in the economic sphere, and quite weak in terms of ideological power.

But it doesn't seem that the economic power of the European Union will expand or dominate in the future. On the contrary, the question arises of how to feed West European (post-colonial) ambitions within such negative dynamics.

Inclusive European security?

Peace is not just any value; it is a precondition for social and moral values to exist. We can hardly have any 'European values' in conditions of war. War has its own values and rules. To prevent war should be the principle aim and crucial leftist strategy. In its historical origins, the European Union was the project against a new great power war in Europe. The last two wars, with global consequences, proved roads to catastrophe. But the European Union was based far less on rejection of Eurocentrism as an instrument for Western hegemony with its universalist designs. On the other hand, it is clearly necessary to find a fragile compromise between diversity in the world and nurturing liberal and socially progressive values at home, i.e. in the European Union.

The Great Recession of 2007-2009 was a typical capitalist crisis, which contributed to the crisis of the West and the European Union. This is a structural crisis of course, not just a crisis of hegemony. Recently, with the growth of populist backlash in the EU (and the USA), talk is more focused on inclusivity. What about peace and inclusive security architecture?

Security is a network of asymmetric relations and interdependencies. It is virtually impossible to enforce or warrant security at someone's expense and then expect there to be no consequences. It is even more naïve or arrogant to blame the consequences on the failure to warrant the secure environment. To claim that US-led NATO is not a reason but a remedy for insecurity in Europe is demagogy.

Europe, as a subcontinent of Eurasia, needs a new security paradigm which is inclusive and not strictly exclusive, based on normative power of the weakening West – be the same or stay outside as *Hannibal ante Portas*. Western Europe (the Atlantic core of the European Union) needs to ponder its own historical situation with new shifts on a global scale and the rise of Asia, considering how to adjust to the world of hybrids. Russia is just one of them, only located in the direct (not just geographical) proximity. In terms of military force, it is still a relevant actor on the continent.

As I have already mentioned, it is not possible to ponder the European security system in terms of ideological kinship, such as liberal EUrope and liberal Russia. EUrope must realise that it is hybrid Russia, both politically and culturally, which will be its partner. It must find a real value in the *Realpolitik*, as an instrument to achieve liberal (not neoliberal!) goals, including balance and equilibrium in a complex world that does not revolve around universally accepted Western values.[13] Russia ponders its own security in classical terms and acts as a great power (although peripheral) with pragmatic approaches. It considers capabilities, not intentions, while EUropean politics is all about good intentions linked to the powerful self-representation of a 'rightful' and liberal EUrope. The paradox is that confrontation with Russia does not make the EU stronger.

If EUrope wants to be relevant as a global actor and not as a global object, it can hardly continue to follow the strategy of Eurocentric predominance. To follow the Eurocentric path in a direct alliance with destructive neoliberal capitalism is not the way to secure the future. Instead, it is a way to continue to weaken internally and sow conflict or war. Ending strife with Russia is just a beginning to start to reform the European Union and make it more open to its own continental diversity, overcoming imperial borders that still divide Europe, not just on a symbolic level.

Of course, there are many constraints. The radical Left is under-represented in recent post-democracy and can only push new foreign political agendas with great difficulty. But we must still try to discuss publicly new issues such as democratisation of foreign policy, promoting dialogue across cultural and other differences, and pondering a new and more just global order, so as to influence public opinion.

But one must be a realist rather than an idealist. The limits are those imposed by US interest in Europe, its military predominance, and EU dependency on Washington. The US is clearly the most powerful state in the world in terms of military capabilities and Trump does not intend to sit back on its hegemonic status. Rather, it represents politics in search of redefinition, based on calculations and externalisation of high hegemonic expenses.

On the other hand, Russia should be seen as a great power pragmatist with many internal weaknesses and a power which is a composite part of *Finis Europae*. This means that there is no reason to underestimate Russia, but we must also understand that power gravity is moving to the East and outside Europe. So far, due to recent confrontation with the West, Russia moves towards rising China. Is this strategically advantageous for the European Union?

Thus, building European security beyond NATO will be a very complicated process that involves not only strategy but also classical diplomacy. It includes deals based on compromises with the USA on the left and Russia on the right. Of course, it does not mean that the USA could and would stay out. Nevertheless, new inclusive security architecture in Europe without NATO is the only real way to restart and change the essence of relations with Russia on the common continent. In fact, this topic represents a key point on the European Union's radical reform agenda. And I am afraid that for the EU there are not many choices left. It is either *reform or perish*.

With grateful acknowledgements to TRANSFORM, the European network for alternative thinking and political dialogue.

www.transform-network.net/publications/issue/inclusive-european-security-russia-and-the-eu-in-the-post-western-world/

Notes

1 Veronika Sušová-Salminen, MA, Ph.D. is a Czech comparative historian and political analyst based in Finland. Her specialisation is Central East Europe and Russia. In 2015, she published the Czech monography about Putin's Russia and its politics. She is an editor of new Czech analytical website !Argument.

2 See for example: Martin Malia, *Russia under Western Eyes: From the Bronze Horseman to the Lenin Mausoleum*, Belnap Press, Harvard 2000, Paul Sanders, Under Western Eyes.

'How meta-narrative shapes our perception of Russia – and why it is time for a qualitative shift,' online: http://www.iwm.at/transit/transit-online/under western-eyes/.

3 See for example: Dmitri Trenin, *Should We Fear Russia?*, Polity Press: London 2016.

4 Reuters: 'Bracing for Russian Military Exercise, Lithuania Puts Up a Border Fence', online: http://www.reuters.com/article/us-lithuania-russia-fence-idUSKBN18W237, Business Insider: 'A nation bordering Russia is building a fence along a third of its border,' online: http://www.businessinsider.com/latvia-border-fence-russia-2015-12.

5 József Böröcz, 'Goodness is Elsewhere: The Rule of European Difference.' *Comparative Studies in Society and History,* pp. 110-138, 2006. Available at SSRN: https://ssrn.com/abstract=1082435

6 Richard Sakwa, 'The Death of Europe? Continental Fates after Ukraine,' in *International Affairs* 91: 3/2015, pp. 553-579.

7 John J. Mearsheimer: *The Tragedy of Great Powers Politics*, W.W. Norton & Company: New York – London 2013.

8 Compare with Andrei: P. Tsygankov, *Russophobia Anti-Russian Lobby and American Foreign Policy*, Macmillan: New York 2009.

9 Jeff D. Colgan – Robert O. Keohane, 'Is Liberal Order Rigged. Fix it now, or Watch it Whither,' in *Foreign Affairs* Vol 96, N. 3, May/June 2017, online: https://www.foreignaffairs.com/articles/world/2017-04-17/liberal-order-rigged

10 Reuters: 'U.S., partners plan European military exercise with 25,000 troops,' online: http://www.reuters.com/article/us-usa-military-europe-idUSKBN18Y23Q

11 For general understanding: Robert Jervis: 'Cooperation Under Security Dilemma,' in *World Politics*, vol. 30, no. 2, 1978, pp. 167–214. JSTOR, www.jstor.org/stable/2009958.

12 See Andrea Komlosy, 'Prospects of Decline and Hegemonic Shifts for the West,' in *Journal of World-Systems Research*, Vol. 22, Issue 2, 2016, pp. 463-483.

13 John Bew, *Realpolitik. A History*. Oxford University Press: London-New York 2016.

Ireland welcomes
Treaty banning nuclear weapons

The President of Ireland, Michael D. Higgins, welcomed the opening up for signature of the Treaty on the Prohibition of Nuclear Weapons, the world's first legally-binding treaty prohibiting the development, testing, manufacturing, purchasing or possessing of nuclear weapons. President Higgins described it as 'a necessary re-affirmation by the representatives of the people of the world of their abhorrence of the continued threat of nuclear weapons.'

'The Treaty on the Prohibition of Nuclear Weapons, adopted in July this year and now formally signed by a large number of UN member states, marks both a significant moment in history and a highpoint of international cooperation. As President of Ireland, I welcome the adoption of this Treaty banning the development, testing, manufacturing, purchasing or possessing of nuclear weapons. From the outset of its membership of the United Nations, Ireland has been a lead country in promoting and advocating the implementation of the Nuclear Non-Proliferation Treaty.

The Treaty on the Prohibition of Nuclear Weapons is the result of decades' worth of work by a number of determined countries, among which Ireland played a prominent role. I salute all those countries in the Core Group of States who initiated this process. That they did so in close cooperation with activists and researchers in civil society organisations around the world is a further ground for hope.

The adoption and coming into force of the Treaty marks the widespread acceptance of the threat to humanity posed by nuclear weapons. Those critics who have opposed and decried this Treaty as being without merit unless it had the assent of those who insist on retaining nuclear weapons are suggesting little less than a veto for the existing nuclear powers on policy making in this area.

I warmly congratulate the Department of Foreign Affairs and Trade for its determined and sustained commitment to this Treaty and its resolute openness and cooperation with a wide range of civil society actors.'

September 2017

NATO forever?

Bertrand Russell

First published in March 1968, this essay asks a pertinent question.

The opening of the Cold War is now beginning to receive the critical attention that it deserves. Until recently, the fervour of the religious crusade kept most of us orthodox. I like to think that my own attitudes have been not untypical. In the period before Hungary and Suez, the late Isaac Deutscher used to visit me at my home in Richmond. I would sit silently as he propounded his views on the Cold War. His scrupulous weighing of the evidence and his balanced presentation of opposing views were always scholarly, but I remained unconvinced. For me, Stalin's terror and the introduction of the one-party state throughout eastern Europe, following the purges and mock trials of the thirties, made unorthodoxy unpalatable, even unthinkable.

Ten years later, however, Deutscher was more persuasive. At a 'teach-in' at Berkeley, California, in May 1965, he summarised[1] his view of the Cold War. Russia had lost 20 million dead in the Second World War and countless million wounded. The war had been fought over its territory, backwards and forwards, with a ferocity unknown in the west, and its industry and economy were in ruins. This was the nation supposedly poised to overrun the rest of Europe to the Atlantic!

Deutscher was more persuasive because, as Stalin receded into history, he was able to quote more authoritative western sources. Ten days before his speech at Berkeley, a lecture[2] had been delivered by George F. Kennan at the Graduate Institute of International Studies in Geneva. Kennan, at the US Embassy in Moscow until 1946, advocate of the containment of Russia and director of the policy planning staff of the State Department, was a leading architect of the theory which called NATO into being. 'After the Second World War,' said Kennan at Geneva, 'American policy-makers could see communism only in terms of a military threat. In creating NATO ... they had drawn a line arbitrarily across Europe against an attack no one was planning ... After the war, the Soviet Union did not want to overrun other countries ... The Atlantic Pact was unfortunate because it was quite unnecessary ... It was perfectly clear to anyone with even a rudimentary knowledge of the Russia of that day, that the Soviet leaders had no intention of attempting to advance their cause by launching military attacks with their own armed forces across frontiers.' NATO could have been conceived, thought Kennan, only by 'people capable of envisaging a favourable future for Europe only along the lines of a total military defeat of the Soviet Union or of some spectacular, inexplicable and wholly improbable collapse of the political will of its leaders.' NATO, according to Kennan, was addressed to the wrong problem. It had 'added depth and recalcitrance to the division of the continent and virtually forced individual countries to choose sides.' From the time of its formation, 'the peaceful solution of Europe's greatest problems on any basis other than that of the permanent division of Germany and the continent, with the implied consignment of the eastern European peoples to inclusion for an indefinite period in the Soviet sphere of power, became theoretically almost inconceivable ... The problem of German unification, the removal of the division of the continent generally, the reintegration of the peoples of central and eastern Europe into the European community ... all these great objectives, vital to any hopeful vision of Europe's future as also to the prospects for world peace, were sacrificed at a stroke.'

Kennan's career underlines the full weight of his criticisms. Nearly all of his life as a professional diplomat has been spent in central and eastern Europe, or in Washington. In April 1947 he was chosen by Secretary of State Marshall to create a new department for the formulation of foreign policy.

Making full use of Kennan's admissions, Deutscher went on at Berkeley to argue that the Truman doctrine and NATO, which proclaimed itself concerned for freedom, had hastened the Stalinization of eastern Europe. The ejection of communists from the governments of France and Italy had preceded Stalin's creation of a single-party system in eastern Europe. Stalin, for all the horrors of his rule, was profoundly conservative, particularly in foreign affairs.

Lord Ismay, an early secretary-general of NATO, sought to dismiss all this. In his book *NATO, the First Five Years, 1949-54*, he opened his first chapter with an account of the Kremlin's 'expansionist policies'. Under this heading he listed such items as the Vietnamese resistance to French attempts to regain control of Vietnam after World War Two. With the United States paying up to 80 per cent of the French colonial war effort in Indo-China, Lord Ismay had no difficulty in detecting Soviet expansionism.

The Truman doctrine of March 1947, which NATO inherited, declared America's will to 'support' and 'assist' what it called 'free peoples'. In his memoirs[3] published recently, Kennan comments: 'since almost no country was without a communist minority, this assumption carried very far.' This is the diplomat's cautious recognition that the Truman doctrine announced America's determination to interfere in the internal affairs of other nations as it chose, in the name of freedom. Kennan, moreover, admits that his famous 'X' article in *Foreign Affairs* in July 1947, which discussed the containment of Russia, had been written two months before the Truman doctrine was launched.

If NATO was, according to Kennan, misconceived 20 years ago, today it is quite unintelligible. Over the past five years we have been taught that the great source of evil in the world is no longer the Soviet Union but China. It is China that features in every discussion of US missile policy and China's embryonic nuclear weapons that 'threaten the world'. This is the moment at which Britain's Prime Minister announces the intended military withdrawal from east of Suez and the limitation of British military power to Europe. This proposed withdrawal from Asia, welcome in itself, although made for the wrong reasons, is quite at variance with what we are told to believe about the menace of China.

Opponents of colonialism cannot fail to notice that an important part of NATO activity is the support of the remnants of European colonialism. Algeria's one million dead testified to the proportions of American aid to France. Today Portugal is wholly dependent upon American assistance through NATO in its attempt to preserve its African empire. It is ironic that Portugal, a ruthless dictatorship, should be a founder-member of NATO, whose spokesman prate about the 'free world' and opposition to totalitarianism. In the same way, the Greek military dictatorship is a child of NATO, which put a gloss of supposed respectability on the mass arrests and tortures inflicted by the new regime.

If we wish to be associated with the increasingly aggressive policies of the American empire, we should have no illusions about the response we shall meet. Every 'hawk' in Washington has his counterpart, and it is idle to suppose that belligerency provokes a will to seek agreement. It is instructive to recall that Khrushchev fell from power in 1964 only weeks after the United States began its bombing attacks on North Vietnam. Khrushchev, who had been at pains to convince his colleagues in the Kremlin that they could come to an understanding with America in the name of peaceful co-existence, had the carpet pulled from under him. If America had wanted to sabotage the possibility of agreement with Russia, the bombing of North Vietnamese ports in the Tonkin Gulf was all that was necessary.

There is a danger that those who watch with horror the barbarism of the United States in Vietnam, and the nauseous opportunism of Wilson and George Brown, may feel that this is nevertheless something remote from their lives. That is not so. We in Western Europe are the allies and hosts of that same America. As long as we are tied by treaty, we are the active accomplices of war criminals. It is a sad reflection on the brutality of our times that it is necessary to argue the case for an absolute dissociation from aggression, indiscriminate slaughter and experimental warfare. Only 20 years ago we hanged men at Nuremburg for such crimes. Today our Government applauds them.

Early next year, membership of the North Atlantic Treaty Organisation will be reviewed under Article 13 of the treaty. This states that 'after the treaty has been in force for 20 years, any party may cease to be a party one year after its notice of denunciation has been given to the government of the United States of America'. The Wilson Government, to judge by its performance since 1964, must hope to confirm its membership without discussion. Whenever a general election is announced, we are assured by the Labour Party that support for the United Nations is the cornerstone of its foreign policy. Before Vietnam, Santo Domingo, Aden and apartheid, we heard much of this from Harold Wilson. It is clear that it is not UN but NATO which determines and dominates the foreign policy of Britain and of all the junior members of the American alliance. There are now important campaigns in several western European nations to withdraw from the organisation, though little of this is reflected in the British Press. I should like to see a similar campaign in Britain, and I see no reason why it should not be supported by a united peace movement and all in the Labour Party who are not craven supporters of Washington. If Britain were to choose to stay in NATO next year, it would lose the opportunity of an independent foreign policy for a further decade or two. Is this really what we want?

The North Atlantic Treaty Article 13
After the Treaty has been in force for twenty years, any Party may cease to be a Party one year after its notice of denunciation has been given to the Government of the United States of America, which will inform the Governments of the other Parties of the deposit of each notice of denunciation.

Notes
1 Published in *Containment and Revolution*, ed. Horowitz (Blond).
2 *Philosophy and Strategy in America's Post-War Policy*, May 11, 1965
3 George F. Kennan, *Memoirs, 1925-1950* (Atlantic-Little, Brown)

Pugwash's London address

The killing of history

John Pilger

John Pilger takes a timely look at Vietnam on TV.

One of the most hyped 'events' of American television, The Vietnam War, has started on the PBS network. The directors are Ken Burns and Lynn Novick. Acclaimed for his documentaries on the Civil War, the Great Depression and the history of jazz, Burns says of his Vietnam films, 'They will inspire our country to begin to talk and think about the Vietnam war in an entirely new way'.

In a society often bereft of historical memory and in thrall to the propaganda of its 'exceptionalism', Burns' 'entirely new' Vietnam war is presented as 'epic, historic work'. Its lavish advertising campaign promotes its biggest backer, Bank of America, which in 1971 was burned down by students in Santa Barbara, California, as a symbol of the hated war in Vietnam.

Burns says he is grateful to 'the entire Bank of America family' which 'has long supported our country's veterans'. Bank of America was a corporate prop to an invasion that killed perhaps as many as four million Vietnamese and ravaged and poisoned a once bountiful land. More than 58,000 American soldiers were killed, and around the same number are estimated to have taken their own lives.

I watched the first episode in New York. It leaves you in no doubt of its intentions right from the start. The narrator says the war 'was begun in good faith by decent people out of fateful misunderstandings, American overconfidence and Cold War misunderstandings'.

The dishonesty of this statement is not surprising. The cynical fabrication of 'false flags' that led to the invasion of Vietnam is a matter of record – the Gulf of Tonkin 'incident' in 1964, which Burns promotes as true, was just one. The lies litter a multitude of official documents, notably the Pentagon Papers, which the great whistleblower Daniel Ellsberg released in 1971.

There was no good faith. The faith was rotten and cancerous. For me – as it must be for many Americans – it is difficult to watch the film's jumble of 'red peril' maps, unexplained interviewees, ineptly cut archive and maudlin American battlefield sequences.

In the series' press release in Britain – the BBC will show it – there is no mention of Vietnamese dead, only Americans. 'We are all searching for some meaning in this terrible tragedy,' Novick is quoted as saying. How very post-modern. All this will be familiar to those who have observed how the American media and popular culture behemoth has revised and served up the great crime of the second half of the twentieth century: from *The Green Berets* and *The Deer Hunter* to *Rambo* and, in so doing, has legitimised subsequent wars of aggression. The revisionism never stops and the blood never dries. The invader is pitied and purged of guilt, while 'searching for some meaning in this terrible tragedy'. Cue Bob Dylan: 'Oh, where have you been, my blue-eyed son?'

I thought about the 'decency' and 'good faith' when recalling my own first experiences as a young reporter in Vietnam: watching hypnotically as the skin fell off Napalmed peasant children like old parchment, and the ladders of bombs that left trees petrified and festooned with human flesh. General William Westmoreland, the American commander, referred to people as 'termites'.

In the early 1970s, I went to Quang Ngai province, where in the village of My Lai, between 347 and 500 men, women and infants were murdered by American troops (Burns prefers 'killings'). At the time, this was presented as an aberration: an 'American tragedy' (*Newsweek*). In this one province, it was estimated that 50,000 people had been slaughtered during the era of American 'free fire zones'. Mass homicide. This was not news.

To the north, in Quang Tri province, more bombs were dropped than in all of Germany during the Second World War. Since 1975, unexploded ordnance has caused more than 40,000 deaths in mostly 'South Vietnam', the country America claimed to 'save' and, with France, conceived as a singularly imperial ruse.

The 'meaning' of the Vietnam war is no different from the meaning of the genocidal campaign against the Native Americans, the colonial massacres in the Philippines, the atomic bombings of Japan, the levelling of every city in North Korea. The aim was described by Colonel Edward Lansdale, the famous CIA man on whom Graham Greene based his central character in *The Quiet American*.

Quoting Robert Taber's *War of the Flea*, Lansdale said, 'There is only one means of defeating an insurgent people who will not surrender, and that is extermination. There is only one way to control a territory that harbours resistance, and that is to turn it into a desert.'

Nothing has changed. When Donald Trump addressed the United Nations on 19 September 2017 – a body established to spare humanity the 'scourge of war' – he declared he was 'ready, willing and able' to 'totally destroy' North Korea and its 25 million people. His audience gasped, but Trump's language was not unusual. His rival for the presidency, Hillary Clinton, had boasted she was prepared to 'totally obliterate' Iran, a nation of more than 80 million people. This is the American Way; only the euphemisms are missing now.

Returning to the US, I am struck by the silence and the absence of an opposition – on the streets, in journalism and the arts, as if dissent once tolerated in the 'mainstream' has regressed to a dissidence: a metaphoric underground. There is plenty of sound and fury at Trump the odious one, the 'fascist', but almost none at Trump the symptom and caricature of an enduring system of conquest and extremism.

Where are the ghosts of the great anti-war demonstrations that took over Washington in the 1970s? Where is the equivalent of the Freeze Movement that filled the streets of Manhattan in the 1980s, demanding that President Reagan withdraw battlefield nuclear weapons from Europe?

The sheer energy and moral persistence of these great movements largely succeeded; by 1987, Reagan had negotiated with Mikhail Gorbachev an Intermediate-Range Nuclear Forces Treaty (INF) that effectively ended the Cold War.

Today, according to secret NATO documents obtained by the German newspaper *Suddeutsche Zeitung*, this vital treaty is likely to be abandoned as 'nuclear targeting planning is increased'. The German Foreign Minister Sigmar Gabriel has warned against 'repeating the worst mistakes of the Cold War … All the good treaties on disarmament and arms control from Gorbachev and Reagan are in acute peril. Europe is threatened again with becoming a military training ground for nuclear weapons. We must raise our voice against this.'

But not in America. The thousands who turned out for Senator Bernie Sanders' 'revolution' in last year's presidential campaign are collectively mute on these dangers. That most of America's violence across the world has been perpetrated not by Republicans, or mutants like Trump, but by liberal Democrats, remains a taboo.

Barack Obama provided the apotheosis, with seven simultaneous wars, a presidential record, including the destruction of Libya as a modern state. Obama's overthrow of Ukraine's elected government has had the desired effect: the massing of American-led NATO forces on Russia's western borderland through which the Nazis invaded in 1941. Obama's 'pivot to Asia' in 2011 signalled the transfer of the majority of America's naval and air forces to Asia and the Pacific for no purpose other than to confront and provoke China. The Nobel Peace Laureate's worldwide campaign of assassinations is arguably the most extensive campaign of terrorism since 9/11.

What is known in the US as 'the left' has effectively allied with the darkest recesses of institutional power, notably the Pentagon and the CIA, to see off a peace deal between Trump and Vladimir Putin and to reinstate Russia as an enemy, on the basis of no evidence of its alleged interference in the 2016 presidential election.

The true scandal is the insidious assumption of power by sinister war-making vested interests for which no American voted. The rapid ascendancy of the Pentagon and the surveillance agencies under Obama represented an historic shift of power in Washington. Daniel Ellsberg rightly called it a coup. The three generals running Trump are its witness.

All of this fails to penetrate those 'liberal brains pickled in the formaldehyde of identity politics', as Luciana Bohne noted memorably. Commodified and market-tested, 'diversity' is the new liberal brand, not the class people serve regardless of their gender and skin colour: not the responsibility of all to stop a barbaric war to end all wars.

'How did it fucking come to this?' says Michael Moore in his Broadway show, *Terms of My Surrender*, a vaudeville for the disaffected set against a backdrop of Trump as Big Brother. I admired Moore's film *Roger & Me*, about the economic and social devastation of his hometown of Flint, Michigan, and *Sicko*, his investigation into the corruption of healthcare in America. The night I saw his show, his happy-clappy audience cheered his reassurance that 'we are the majority!' and calls to 'impeach Trump, a liar and a fascist!' His message seemed to be that had you held your nose and voted for Hillary Clinton, life would be predictable again. He may be right. Instead of merely abusing the world, as Trump does, the Great Obliterator might have attacked Iran and lobbed missiles at Putin, whom she likened to Hitler: a particular profanity given the 27 million Russians who died in Hitler's invasion.

'Listen up,' said Moore, 'putting aside what our governments do, Americans are really loved by the world!'

There was a silence.

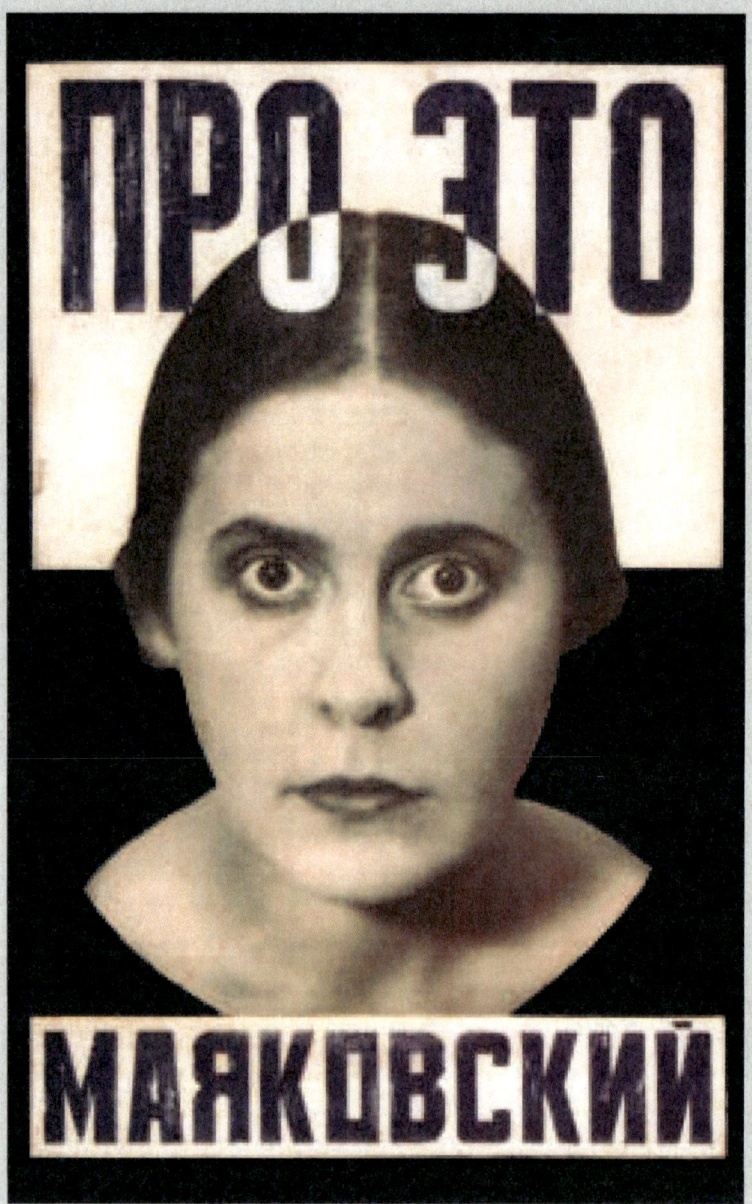

Cover for Mayakovsky's 'About This' with Lili Brik, 1923 (see p.118)

From Vladimir Lenin to Vladimir Putin

100 Years of The October Revolution in Russia

*Roy Medvedev
and
Zhores Medvedev*

This centenary essay by two foremost historians of modern Russia is published there in a history journal and, in shorter version, in some Russian newspapers. It is also included in volumes for two large international forums on the Revolution, one in Moscow on 3 to 6 November 2017, and the other in St Petersburg a few days earlier.

Russia before 1917

In 1914, Russia's population was 171 million people, significantly exceeding that of the United States (99 million), not to mention the economically developed countries of Europe. In terms of national income, Russia was fourth in the world, behind the US, Germany and Britain. Of the other world powers, France, Italy, Austria-Hungary and Japan ranked in 5th, 6th, 7th and 8th places. But in terms of income per capita, Russia lagged behind all major European countries, although it was ahead of Japan.

The welfare of Britain, France, Spain, Holland, Belgium and Portugal was ensured by the exploitation of considerable natural resources in their numerous colonies in Africa, in Asia and in South America. Germany (which in terms of its industrial development was leading in Europe), though it was called an 'empire', had almost no colonies, which significantly limited its economic prospects. The violent redistribution of colonial possessions that began at the end of the 19th century, however, was initiated in Asia by Japanese aggression against China, followed in 1904 by Japan's attack on Russia, which ended in the loss of South Sakhalin and Port Arthur.

At the beginning of the 20th century, Russia remained an agrarian country, and its predominantly peasant population was united in communities for joint ownership of land. This system, which had existed for hundreds of years and sustained villages in difficult climatic conditions, was destroyed by the reforms of Prime Minister Pyotr Stolypin, who introduced private ownership of land and allowed peasant households to leave the community and create farms. Stolypin's reforms quickly increased agricultural productivity. By the beginning of 1914, Russia had become the largest grain exporter in Europe. There was rapid development of cities and industry.

Russia's participation in the war with Austria-Hungary and Germany, which broke out in August 1914, was determined by its allied commitments and not by Russia's national interests. The Russian army was the largest in Europe. But by the end of 1916, its losses amounted to 3.6 million killed, more than two million prisoners, and millions of wounded. Defeats in the war, and occupation by the German and Austrian armies of Poland, Ukraine and the Baltic, led to a sharp decline in food supply to Petrograd, at that time not only Russia's capital but also the main industrial centre. At the end of 1916, the city's population was approaching 3 million people. Rapid inflation and a sharp decline in the purchasing power of the rouble caused serious problems in providing food to Petrograd, which was connected to the south of the country by only one railway. Hunger riots, strikes and demonstrations began in the capital. Peasants in the south of the country refused to sell grain for depreciated roubles.

The February Revolution

The general strike of workers in Petrograd, which began on 23 February (8 March, according to the Gregorian calendar introduced later), spread to hundreds of factories. Barricades appeared on the streets of the proletarian districts of the capital. During the following days, many military units of the garrison began to shift to the side of the workers. The events of this period are described quite well not only by day, but even by hour. On 1 March (14), the Provisional Government of Russia was formed. Tsar Nicholas II's renunciation of the throne was signed and announced on 2 March (15) 1917, and was met with universal rejoicing throughout Russia. It was the Provisional Government that carried out the country's main reforms: the abolition of the death penalty, the dissolution of the gendarmerie, equal rights for all citizens, the abolition of the privileges of the nobility, the abolition of the 'table of ranks' for civil servants and the military, the amnesty of political prisoners and emigrants, and many others.

The revolutionary movement in Russia might have waned if the new democratic government had decided to withdraw from the war and negotiate peace with Germany and Austria-Hungary. This, however, did not happen, although the Russian army was falling apart. Russia's Provisional Government, mainly under pressure from French and British allies, decided to continue the war 'to a victorious end'. The offensive launched at the front ended in defeat.

The second critical problem was the financial one. Russia could survive the fall of the monarchy, but she could not survive the fall of the 'royal' rouble. Before the war, not only paper notes with the tsars' images were printed. There were also minted gold coins, worth ten and five roubles; minted silver coins worth one rouble, and denominations of 50, 25, 15, 10 and 5 kopeks; kopeks and ½ kopeks were minted from copper. The presence of gold and silver coins in circulation reliably ensured the circulation of paper banknotes, of which the highest at par value was the 500 rouble note depicting Peter the Great. From 1915, inflation associated with the war led to the disappearance from circulation not only of gold and silver but also copper coins. They stopped minting. The government printed large amounts of paper notes. After the February Revolution, banknotes with images of tsars rapidly lost their 'pecuniary' status and were withdrawn from circulation. They were replaced by new banknotes, which the people called *'kerenki'*, after Prime Minister A F Kerensky. These notes were printed on bad paper and did not have numbers and signatures. Provision of *kerenki*, harvesting food, supplies to cities and ordinary trade all proved difficult. In autumn, with the onset of cold weather, hunger was again Petrograd's main problem. Moscow, which had a knot of eight railways, survived due to natural commodity exchange.

The October Revolution

The October Revolution – the overthrow of the Provisional Government, and the transfer of power in the capital to the Military Revolutionary Committee of the Petrograd Soviet of Workers' and Soldiers' Deputies – was bloodless. Late in the evening of 25 October (7 November), the Second All-Russia Congress of Soviets of Workers 'and Soldiers' Deputies, in which the Bolsheviks and Left Socialist-Revolutionaries had a majority, proclaimed the transfer of power to the Soviets in Petrograd and throughout Russia. The Congress adopted not only the Decree on Peace, but also the Decree on Land, the main provision of which was the confiscation of landlord property to be transferred to the peasants. The Congress formed the new government of Russia – the Council of People's Commissars (SNK), headed by Vladimir Ulyanov (Lenin). The government included L D Bronstein (Trotsky) as the People's Commissar for Foreign Affairs, and I V Dzhugashvili (Stalin) as People's Commissar for Nationalities.

The Brest Peace Treaty with Germany, signed in early March 1918 after the successful offensive of the German army, was essentially a surrender of Russia, which lost vast western territories, including Ukraine. The Brest

Peace was, however, annulled in November 1918 after the surrender of Germany and Austria-Hungary in the war on the Western Front.

Civil War

The civil war in Russia began only a year after the October Revolution. Hundreds of books have been written about this war. There are dozens of interpretations of its causes and consequences. The most important is the indisputable fact that it was the Bolsheviks, and the Workers' and Peasants' Red Army (RKKA) that they created, which won in this long war a victory that consolidated disintegrating Russia and transformed it into a new federal state, the Union of Soviet Socialist Republics (USSR). The 'New Economic Policy' (NEP) played a significant role in this victory. It was announced at the Tenth Congress of the Russian Communist Party (Bolshevik) (RCP (B)), replacing the policy of 'war communism'.

New Economic Policy

Russia's economic situation in 1921 can be characterized by one word: ruin. The territory of Russia, controlled by the Bolshevik government, declined as a result of Finland, Estonia, Latvia, Lithuania, Poland, and Bessarabia breaking away from the Russian Empire. Poland annexed the western regions of Belorussia and Ukraine, occupied by the Polish army. A significant reduction in Russia's indigenous population was associated with losses in the Civil War, famine, epidemics and emigration. According to rough estimates, about 130 million people lived in the USSR in 1922.

The introduction of the New Economic Policy saved the country from economic ruin. New laws allowed private entrepreneurship and trade. Destructive interventions in agriculture were replaced by a tax in kind, which stimulated agricultural production. The development of market relations began with a financial reform – the introduction of 'chervontsi' *guaranteed* with gold, silver roubles and fifty kopeks. In the extraction of minerals and in industry, 'concessions' – leasing to foreign companies and firms of mines and factories – were allowed. The banking system revived. The country's economy developed at a rapid pace. In 1928, national income grew by 18 per cent. In comparison with Western countries, which fell victim to difficult economic crisis in 1928, the Soviet Union stood out for its achievements.

Vladimir Lenin

Lenin was the leader and organiser of the October Revolution. Returning from exile to Petrograd in early April 1917, Lenin published in *Pravda* his famous 'April Theses', which substantiated the need for the bourgeois-democratic revolution to grow into a socialist revolution, 'during which power must pass into the hands of the proletariat and the poorest peasantry'. This programme was a new doctrine that contradicted the basic postulates of Marxism. In conditions of continuing war and the food crisis, however, there were chances of success.

The October Revolution did not change the critical food situation in the capital. The German army's offensive against Petrograd continued, threatening Narva and Pskov. Finland announced its independence, its border with Russia in the southern part of the Karelian isthmus just 30 km from Petrograd. During the winter, the supply of food to Petrograd was hampered and bread rations for the population were reduced to 120-200 grams per day. State employees, bank employees, post and telegraph employees, without receiving cash wages, refused to go to work.

An historic solution to this critical situation was found. On 13 March 1918, the Council of People's Commissars secretly decided to move the capital of the Russian Republic from Petrograd to Moscow. The Moscow Kremlin became the residence of the Soviet government.

However, Lenin himself often neglected security measures. At rallies in the factories, he often went by car only with the chauffeur. On 30 August 1918 at one of the factories in Moscow, Lenin was seriously wounded after an attempt on his life by the Socialist-Revolutionary Kaplan. By late October, Lenin had recovered sufficiently to resume his work and speeches. However, there was no complete recovery. Lenin's state of health worsened. The last time he worked in his office in the Kremlin was on 12 December 1922.

Joseph Stalin

Lenin was not a dictator, he was a leader. There was a 'dictatorship of the Bolshevik Party', in the shape of its Central Committee and the Politburo. In his December 1922 'Letter to the Congress', which he dictated realising that his days were numbered, Lenin gave brief descriptions of six of his closest associates, Stalin, Trotsky, Zinoviev, Kamenev, Bukharin and Pyatakov, noting their positive and negative qualities. The choice of a new leader of the Party was proposed to the next Congress. At the Thirteenth Congress of the RCP (B) in May 1924, the delegates decided on Stalin. Trotsky, with his idea of 'permanent revolution', was considered too radical.

The Communist Party in Russia, and then the USSR, through acquiring the monopoly of power via the liquidation of all other political groups, gradually transformed itself into a governing system which, many years later, the Yugoslav communist Milovan Djilas defined as a 'new class'.

> '... The case was the reverse with new classes in the Communist systems. It did not come to power to *complete* a new economic order but to *establish* its own and, in so doing, to establish its power over society.'

Djilas' formulations reflected the new policy in the USSR begun by Stalin to industrialise the country and collectivise its peasant population, accompanied by a terrorist campaign of 'eliminating the kulaks as a class'. These directions of reforms were mutually connected. Collectivising agriculture and removing kulaks from the countryside led to millions of peasants leaving the villages. They were sent, often compulsorily, to construct roads, mines, and plants. Streams of prisoners were sent to especially difficult regions of the Urals, Siberia and the Far East. It was the prisoners who built the White Sea-Baltic Canal, the Moscow-Volga Canal, the Vorkuta and Karaganda coal mines, the Norilsk nickel mines, the Kolyma copper mines, the iron ore mines of Magnitogorsk, the Komsomolsk-on-Amur shipyard, and many other 'shock' five-year building projects. A powerful military industry was also created.

For all these rapid transformations, the monopoly of power of the All Soviet Communist Party (Bolshevik) (VKP (B)) and its discipline proved insufficient. When creating a 'command-administrative' system in the economy, there was a major shift in the system and structure of power in the USSR. Stalin subordinated the Party to punitive organs of the People's Commissariat for Internal Affairs (NKVD). Most of the old guard of the Party were destroyed. Repression affected millions of people and the command of the Red Army. Party ideology was supplemented by the cult of Stalin's personality, and he himself became an unbridled dictator. A regime of totalitarianism, based on mass terror, was established in the country. The weakening of the army as a result of terror was clearly manifested in the Soviet-Finnish war of 1939-1940. The Soviet Union was unprepared for Germany's surprise attack on 22 June 1941.

However, during the war years, the influence and power of punitive agencies and party structures weakened. Military discipline extended to all sectors of society. The level of mobilization of resources and the population for the war was more extensive in the USSR than in Germany. The highest authority was the State Defence Committee. Stalin had full authority as Supreme Commander-in-Chief and Chairman of the Council of People's Commissars. Victory in the war against Germany, and then against Japan, returned to the Soviet Union a number of Russian territories lost in 1905 and in 1918. After the Second World War, Stalin dismissed marshals and generals from power and again prioritised the punitive organs of state. Some mass repressive actions were of ethnic and religious nature. The second most influential man in the country was L P Beria. For the Party nomenclature, beginning with secretaries of the district committees, a secret system of the second higher salary was introduced, 'Stalin's envelopes'.

Nikita Khrushchev

After the death of Stalin, N S Khrushchev, holding the post of secretary of the Central Committee of the Communist Party of the Soviet Union (CPSU), relying on marshals and generals, made a new coup. Beria and his closest associates were arrested and shot, after a closed trial, and power in the country again passed to the party nomenclature. Stalin's main collaborators, Molotov, Voroshilov, Mikoyan, Malenkov and Kaganovich were transferred to secondary posts. Khrushchev's historic speech, 'On the cult of personality and its consequences' at the Twentieth Congress of the CPSU in February 1956, discrediting Stalin's punitive dictatorship, ensured the rehabilitation of millions of convicts and a change in the structure of power. The totalitarian regime was replaced by an authoritarian one. The Committee for State Security (KGB), a smaller version of the Ministry of State Security (MGB), was subordinate to the Presidium of the Central Committee of the CPSU. The layer of privileged Party and Soviet nomenclature again acquired the character of a governing class, and government officials of all levels and enterprise managers submitted to decisions of Party committees. The Party organs became 'directive', the Soviets became 'executive'. 'Stalin's cash envelopes' were abolished as illegal. The high standard of living of the 'new class' was provided not only by increased salaries, but also by numerous privileges (large apartments, state dachas, cars with chauffeurs, special shops, special hospitals, special resorts, etc.).

Industry, especially military-space production, continued to develop, stimulated by the confrontation of the 'Cold War'. However, agriculture entered a period of protracted crisis and the provision of food to cities became dependent on imports.

Leonid Brezhnev

The removal of Khrushchev from all posts at the Plenum of the Central Committee of the CPSU in October 1964 again changed the structure of power in the USSR. The new system of governing the country was now designated a 'collective leadership.' Prime Minister Alexei Kosygin could make independent decisions in this system of government. Mikhail Suslov led ideology and all the press, book publishing, radio and television. Leonid Brezhnev focused on the defence industry, military and international problems. The powers of the KGB were significantly reduced and political repression became limited. A favourable situation for the USSR on world markets, with high oil and natural gas prices, the country's main exports, brought large sums of foreign currency to the Soviet budget. This allowed for a significant increase in the import of food and consumer goods, and stimulated housing construction. An increase in the well-being of the urban population was observed. The collective farm system experienced further decline. This led to the adoption of a new Constitution that equalised the rights of workers and peasants by issuing uniform passports to all citizens of the USSR. The 'new class' of privileged citizens of the country with a high standard of living was significantly expanded. It included not only those working for Party bodies, but also the upper stratum of civil servants, officers and generals of the army, and directors of enterprises. But membership of the CPSU was compulsory. The standard of living of workers, peasants and those in the mass professions remained low. Repressive measures against critics of the regime included deportation and psychiatric 'expertise.' Although the 'Cold War' with the West gave way to 'détente', tension rose in the East in relations with China. The Soviet military machine and arsenal of atomic and thermonuclear bombs and their means of delivery reached parity with NATO.

Yuri Andropov

Yuri Andropov, who headed the KGB from 1967, as a member of the Politburo managed to significantly increase the influence of this organization. Marshal Dmitry Ustinov, appointed to the post of Minister of Defence, had also joined the 'collective leadership' in 1974. Brezhnev's illness, the accidental death in 1980 of Alexei Kosygin, and the death of Mikhail Suslov in 1981, meant that, after Brezhnev's death in 1982, Yuri Andropov became leader of the CPSU. By this time, the 'Brezhnev' leadership of the USSR was deeply corrupted. Andropov, an ideological communist, ascetic and intellectual, made the basis of his policy a decisive fight against corruption in the Party and state apparatus. This made him popular. However, suffering from kidney disease, Andropov died in February 1984. Konstantin Chernenko, who succeeded him as General Secretary, was constantly ill and remained in power for only one year. By that time Dmitry Ustinov had died. The priority of the Party and state elite was to choose a leader from the younger members of the Politburo. At the suggestion of Andrei Gromyko, the most authoritative and influential member of the Politburo at the time, Mikhail Gorbachev was elected as the new General Secretary, although he had then done nothing to distinguish himself. Gorbachev shared power with Gromyko, elected Chairman of the Presidium of the Supreme Soviet of the USSR, and with Nikolai Ryzhkov, appointed to the post of prime minister.

Mikhail Gorbachev

Under Gorbachev, such concepts as *'perestroika'* and *'glasnost'* entered the political lexicon, but the economic policy of the new leader remained a hostage to the decisions of the Brezhnev era. Excess revenues from the export of oil and natural gas since the mid-1970s were viewed as a permanent factor in the world economy. The priority of developing nuclear energy was recognised as a guarantee of economic prosperity. In the Soviet Union, a programme was implemented to increase production and growth of oil and natural gas exports, as well as a long-term programme to construct nuclear power plants, including thermal nuclear in cities. It was assumed that, by the beginning of the new century, nuclear power would account for 50-60 per cent of electricity generation, and almost 50 per cent of budget revenues would come from oil and gas exports.

The Chernobyl disaster in April 1986 caused significant damage to this programme and the country's economy. Construction of almost 60 nuclear power facilities was stopped. Hundreds of thousands of highly qualified people lost their jobs. About a million residents of contaminated areas needed resettlement. Tens of thousands of 'liquidators', mostly military, suffered from radiation. In 1986, due to excess production ('glut'), world oil prices fell two-thirds. This deprived the Soviet Union of most of its export revenues. In late 1988, a powerful earthquake in Armenia led to the deaths and injuries of tens of thousands of people, and the destruction and damage of almost 30 per cent of the buildings in the republic, as well as halting two units of an Armenian nuclear power plant, compounding the complex of economic and humanitarian problems. Personally, Gorbachev was reproached for a failed anti-alcohol campaign launched in 1985.

In 1988, in this crisis situation, Gorbachev carried out the most radical political reform to democratise the country since February 1917. Until 1988 in the Soviet Union there was no reliable system for making laws. The joint decisions of the Central Committee of the CPSU and the Council of Ministers of the USSR had legislative power. The Supreme Council was a decoration and met only for a few days a year to approve the draft budget.

Amendments to the Constitution of 1977 created a super-parliament, 'The Congress of People's Deputies', whose members were elected by district on an alternative basis. The permanent real parliament, the 'Supreme Soviet of the USSR', which was created from among the people's deputies, acquired legislative powers and approved the composition of the government. Elections of people's deputies took place in spring 1989 in two rounds. Roy Medvedev was elected to the Congress of People's Deputies and the Supreme Soviet of the USSR.

The Soviet Union stopped subsidising socialist and communist regimes in other countries; in Ethiopia, Angola, Vietnam, Cuba and Eastern Europe. This led to the collapse of the Council for Mutual Economic Assistance (CMEA) and to the complete end of the Cold War.

In 1990, the post of 'President of the USSR' was created, to which Mikhail Gorbachev was elected by the Congress of People's Deputies.

The new reforms stimulated political activity among broad masses of the population. The CPSU lost its monopoly on power. Soviet citizenship was restored to 'dissidents' who had been expelled from the country. Among them was Zhores Medvedev. New laws permitted private entrepreneurial activity and the creation of productive, service and trade co-operatives.

Decentralization of the country's governance and the democratic creation, in 1990, of permanent Supreme Soviets in all the union and autonomous republics led to the emergence of separatist tendencies in some places. On 12 June 1990, Boris Yeltsin, who was elected chairman of the Congress of People's Deputies of the Russian Soviet Federative Socialist Republic (RSFSR), initiated adoption of the Declaration on State Sovereignty of the RSFSR. This 'Declaration' was the beginning of the collapse of the USSR.

In July 1991, Yeltsin was elected president of the RSFSR. In December, he initiated the agreement to liquidate the USSR and create a 'Commonwealth of Independent States' (CIS). The CIS included 12 of the 15 former union republics. Lithuania, Latvia and Estonia chose full independence. After dismantling the USSR, about 25 million ethnic Russians were left outside their historical homeland and were often subject to discrimination.

Boris Yeltsin

In 1992, after the collapse of the Soviet Union into the Russian Federation and other CIS countries, the main problem was financial. The abolition of 'Soviet' roubles depicting Lenin deprived the population in Russia and in other republics of all their accumulated savings. Inflation of new 'Russian' money was rapid. In the Russian Federation, which became a sovereign state, for almost three years there was a struggle for power between the Congress of People's Deputies and the president. In October 1993, the illegal forced dispersal of the Congress of People's Deputies with the use of tanks, accompanied by a large number of victims, made Yeltsin a temporary dictator. The creation of a 'market economy' in the country and the privatisation of its natural resources and industrial enterprises through 'mortgage auctions' and privatisation vouchers, land privatisation, the dissolution of collective and state farms and many other acts of 'shock therapy' were carried out on the basis of Yeltsin's Decrees. The new Constitution of the Russian Federation, which replaced the Supreme Council by the State Duma and radically increased the powers and authority of the president, was adopted without discussion by referendum in December 1993. Yeltsin, elected in 1991 as president of the RSFSR, then part of the USSR, unaccountably acquired new powers in the now sovereign country without re-election. The presidential elections envisaged by the new Constitution were delayed due to Yeltsin's low rating and were held only in June 1996. In the first round of voting, Yeltsin gained 35 per cent of the vote. Between the first and second rounds Yeltsin was hospitalised with a heart attack. This fact was hidden from the public and Yeltsin's few 'appearances', shown on television, were false.

In the period from 1995 to 1998, President Yeltsin and his 'team' tried quickly to create a new ruling class of millionaires, billionaires and bankers who paid a pittance for public property. They began to be defined by the people as 'oligarchs'. Oligarchic capitalism at the end of the 1990s, represented by Berezovsky, Abramovich, Gusinsky, Potanin, Khodorkovsky, Smolensky, Nevzlin, Aven, and others, had nothing to do with capitalism in Russia until 1917, when the richest people, Demidov, Putilov, Morozov, Ryabushinsky and others, were representatives of the dynasties of entrepreneurs creating a variety of new industries in Russia.

Voucher and collateral privatization, which did not bring real money to the treasury, led to a significant budget deficit. About 60 per cent of the Russian economy was under the control of the oligarchs and a significant part of the profits settled in foreign banks. To generate money, in addition to the printing press, a financial pyramid of state short-term bonds (T-bills) began to be created. This collapsed early in August 1998. The result of the default and government crisis was Yeltsin's forced appointment of

Yevgeny Primakov to the post of Prime Minister. Primakov had variously served as Foreign Minister, former Chief of the First Main Directorate of the USSR KGB, and director of the Foreign Intelligence Service of the Russian Federation (until 1996). Primakov was also a prominent orientalist scholar, member of the Russian Academy of Sciences, and director of the Institute of World Economy and International Relations.

However, it was Primakov's success in overcoming the consequences of the financial and economic crises and the growth of his popularity that led Yeltsin and the oligarchs to unexpectedly and unreasonably dismiss him in May 1999. They tried in this way to deprive him of the chance of a presidential post. The role of Prime Minister was given to Minister of Internal Affairs Sergey Stepashin, who lasted only three months.

Vladimir Putin

Vladimir Putin, lieutenant colonel of the KGB reserve, who replaced as prime minister colonel-general of the Ministry of Internal Affairs Stepashin, headed the Federal Security Service (FSB) from July 1998. Putin was little known and, until 2000, did not hold any elected posts. In late 1999, with the next presidential election approaching in July 2000, Primakov was among the candidates for this post, according to public opinion polls. He was nominated by the party 'Fatherland – All Russia', which had a left-wing orientation. Primakov was ahead of the leader of the Communist Party of the Russian Federation, Gennady Zyuganov, by a small margin. Putin, at that time prime minister, was not in a party and was not nominated as a candidate for president. Meanwhile, the absolute priority for Yeltsin and the oligarchs was to prevent Primakov from coming to power. In this situation, a plan was created for the early voluntary resignation of Yeltsin, as a result of which Vladimir Putin, as prime minister, became constitutional 'acting president' without election, but for a short time. Three months of the presidency and some skilful management of the new war in Chechnya gave Putin the advantage when competing with other candidates. Primakov, the recent favourite of the election campaign, withdrew his candidacy. This provided Putin with victory – 53 per cent of the vote – in the first round.

The Constitution of the Russian Federation, drawn up 'under Yeltsin', endowed the Russian president with more powers than the presidents of the United States, France or China.

Putin, in the first term of his presidency, did not seek to redistribute property. However, he removed the oligarchs from influencing political decisions, subordinating the activities of those who did not go abroad to the interests of the Russian economy. A new ruling party was formed, United Russia, which merged with the Fatherland party. The new party did not have a clear ideological programme. It had a patriotic platform, which provided the president and the government with the support of the majority of deputies in the State Duma and in the Federation Council. In 2004, in the presidential election, the new party nominated Putin. 71 per cent of those who took part in the elections voted for him.

The establishment of a real legislative power in Russia and in its main regions and autonomous republics led to the predominant development of the public sector in the form of joint corporations in the oil and gas industries, in the extraction of natural minerals, in large-scale and military industry, and in foreign trade. Many important enterprises were bought from private owners by the state. Thus, state corporations Rosatom, Rosgidro, Rosset, Rosneft, Gazprom, Rosnano and others emerged. On the basis of production infrastructure inherited from the USSR and its engineering and design personnel, the military industry developed successfully. Russia regained the status of a world military power. Light industry, agriculture and domestic trade remained and developed mainly in the private sector in strong competition with imports. During the 1990s and 'Yeltsin's rule', the standard of living fell almost twofold. This was a bad advertisement for the 'market economy'. During the period 2001-2014, according to the International Statistical Yearbook of the *Encyclopaedia Britannica* for 2016, Russia's gross domestic product per capita increased from $1,750 to $13,200, which, in terms of purchasing power (purchasing power parity, the new index of economic statistics), is $24,710. This was slightly higher than the corresponding index in Poland ($24,090). (In the US, the gross national product (GNP) per capita is $55,860.) Russia's external public debt declined over the same period from $101 billion to $35 billion. (In all states that arose after the collapse of the USSR, public debts increased).

All the problems associated with Putin's new economic and international policies cannot be considered in this brief 'jubilee' essay. You can, however, ask the question, is there a 'new class' in modern Russia? It was definitely formed, and still exists. But this is not a class of the bourgeoisie. The political party of the big bourgeoisie, the Union of Right Forces, transformed in 2008 into the Right Cause party. It has never been able to reach the 5 per cent threshold in elections to the State Duma. Its rating did not exceed two per cent.

There most certainly is a 'new class' in Russia – if we understand by this concept groups of people whose incomes and property values are five to ten times higher than those of workers in industry, agriculture, and those serving in the mass professions: teachers, nurses, public transport workers, trade and others. This middle class consists of state officials, army, navy and law enforcement officers, the judiciary and prosecutor's corps, deputies of the Duma and the Federation Council, and elected bodies in the republics and regions, academicians and artists, small and medium-sized entrepreneurs, and some other categories of citizens.

From political economy it is known that the development of the productive forces of society changes the relations of production. At present, in the highly technological societies of the 21st century, the proletariat and the peasantry, in the forms in which they existed in Russia at the beginning of the 20th century, are no longer there. Political and economic realities, which in 1917 led to two revolutions in Russia, are no longer there. It is the middle class that dominates now in all countries of Europe. In the United States and in its economy and politics, large capital still prevails; one representative of which is its new president, Donald Trump. In the People's Republic of China, power was reformed in the 1970s by the Deng Xiaoping's Communist Party. It created 'socialism with Chinese characteristics.' Oligarchic capitalism has survived in Ukraine and Georgia – authoritarian rule in the Republic of Belarus and in Kazakhstan.

However, we should single out a special group of people as part of the Russian middle class, which can be defined as the 'managing elite'. In general terms, it consists of those officials who are appointed to their posts by presidential decree, decisions of the prime minister, or are elected to posts in legislative bodies, the State Duma and the Federation Council. The ruling elite includes governors of oblasts, presidents of autonomous areas, top ranks in military and law enforcement agencies, the FSB, the Ministry of Internal Affairs, judges, prosecutors, leading employees of the Central Bank and a large number of other departments. The modern state system has a very complex structure.

Russia is not only the largest country in the world; it is also the most complex. The management system in Russia cannot be copied from other countries. There are 85 regions, of which 17 are autonomous republics. In these regions, local languages, Tatar, Bashkir, Chechen, Kalmyk and others have equal status with the Russian. The Christian Orthodox religion, Islam, Buddhism and Judaism are practised freely. The governors of the regions and the presidents of the Russian autonomous areas have more powers to solve major regional problems than party and Soviet administrators in the past. Strong presidential power, like a strong army, is for Russia in these conditions not a defect, but a necessity.

Vladimir Putin's great power relies not only on his broad constitutional competences, but also on the high authority of the national leader and the apparent support of the majority of the population. We can assume that Putin will again be re-elected in 2018 for his final six-year term. The changes that will occur in the management of Russia after 2024 are difficult to predict.

The anniversary of the October Revolution, once the main holiday in the USSR, with parades and demonstrations, is not celebrated in modern Russia. But its 100-year anniversary certainly will not go unnoticed. This revolution was one of the turning points in world history. It had a great influence on the fate of many countries.

Russia's main holiday was the 'Day of the Great Victory'. On the eve of 9 May, every veteran of the war, about a million in 2017, receives at his home address in Russia, or abroad, through embassies, a congratulatory letter signed by the President of the Russian Federation.

The 100th anniversary of the October Revolution is an important historic anniversary, but not a holiday. In fact, nothing is celebrated on this day. The October Revolution changed the course of history, but it did not bring prosperity and justice to the peoples of Russia. In the gigantic political experiments of the peoples of Russia there was no continuity. The New Economic Policy rejected the destructive tendencies of war communism. Stalin's Five-Year Plans buried the achievements of the NEP. Khrushchev's 'thaw' exposed Stalin's terror and the cult of personality. Brezhnev rejected the 'voluntarism' and authoritarianism of Khrushchev. Gorbachev tried to create a socialist democracy. Yeltsin destroyed both socialism and the USSR. The political and economic systems of modern Russia have their beginning in 2000, not 1917. In the development of new technologies, labour productivity, the welfare of the population and simply the health of people and their life expectancy, Russia is not a leader in the modern world. But in the time that has passed since October 1917, Russia and its peoples have acquired colossal political experience. Having the world's largest territory and the richest resources, Russia is far ahead of all other countries of the world in its still unrealised opportunities and prospects.

Roy A. Medvedev, Ph.D., was born in Tbilisi, Georgia in 1925, and educated at Leningrad University. His books in English translation include *Let History Judge: The Origin and Consequences of Stalinism, Khrushchev: The Years in Power, The October Revolution, All Stalin's Men, On Soviet Dissent, Post-Soviet Russia, China and the Superpowers.*

Zhores A.Medvedev, Ph.D., was born in Tbilisi, Georgia in 1925, and educated at Moscow Timiriazev Agriculural Academy. His books in English include *The Rise and Fall of T.D. Lysenko, Medvedev Papers, Soviet Science, Nuclear Disaster in the Urals, Khrushchev: The Years in Power (with Roy Medvedev), Soviet Agriculture, Andropov, Gorbachev. The Legacy of Chernobyl, The Unknown Stalin (with Roy Medvedev).*

Moscow-London, September 2017

Translation prepared by Nicole Morris and Tony Simpson.

Roy (left) and Zhores Medvedev, London, 2003

*Presidium of the Second Northern Oblast Congress of Soviets, 1 August 1918.
Seated: Uritskii, Trotsky, Sverdlov, Zinoviev, and Lashevich. Standing:
Kharitonov, Lisovskii, Korsak, Voskov, Gusev, Ravich, Bakaev, and Kuzmin. St.
Petersburg Institute of History, Russian Academy of Sciences.
(The Bolsheviks in Power, p. 325)*

Bertrand Russell's vital Socialism

Jean Bricmont
&
Normand Baillargeon

Jean Bricmont is a professor of physics at the Université Catholique de Louvain. Normand Baillargeon is a professor of education at the Université du Québec à Montréal. This article is adapted from the preface to a French-language edition of Bertrand Russell's The Practice and Theory of Bolshevism, *published in France by Éditions du Croquant in 2014. Translated from the French by Diana Johnstone. With grateful acknowledgements to the authors, translator and to* Monthly Review.

In 1918, a few days before being jailed for pacifism, Bertrand Russell completed *Proposed Roads to Freedom: Socialism, Anarchism and Syndicalism,* a short, simple, and profound guide to the theories of anarchism, Marxist socialism, anarcho-socialism, and guild socialism – the associative form of socialism that existed in Great Britain in those days.

All those theories called for collective appropriation of the means of production within a democratic framework, which amounts to what could be called nineteenth-century socialism (broader than that of Marx), itself stemming from the ideas of the Enlightenment. Eighteenth-century thinkers sought to emancipate humanity from the constraints of their era: royal absolutism, feudalism, and religious obscurantism. And the solutions they came up with, freedom of expression, separation of powers, and representative democracy, were adequate responses to those problems. It is easy to understand why they were also often in favour of the free market, because they rightly rejected the feudal tolls, which impeded circulation of goods.

But as industry developed, the 'free market' produced a concentration of wealth in a few hands. At the same time, production became *de facto* 'socialized' in the sense of involving many individuals instead of independent producers, requiring infrastructure enabling transport of raw materials and merchandise, and calling for educated workers in reasonably good health. These external social factors are necessary for industrial production.

The basic idea of socialism is that once the production process is in fact socialized, its control should be socialized too, at least if the aspirations for emancipation expressed by eighteenth-century liberalism are to be realised. If the means of production and – as happened in the twentieth century – the means of information are concentrated in a few hands, those who possess them exercise an enormous power over the rest of the population. They can influence elections, either directly by financing candidates, or indirectly by threatening governments that resist their demands with economic reprisals (capital flight, plant delocalisations). These days, weaker countries face the threat of (mainly US) sanctions and military intervention. The disagreements between doctrines discussed in Russell's book deal with what should be done 'after the revolution': what should be the role of the state, how much economic and social constraint should weigh on individuals, and what form of democracy is desirable – direct, representative, or by means of councils representing producers and consumers.

Russell's attitude remains moderate in these debates. Although he appreciates the arguments of pure anarchism, represented by Peter Kropotkin, he considers those ideas too extreme to be put into practice: free goods, total freedom to work or not to work, absence of any governmental constraint. Kropotkin's arguments are always ingenious, but the radical nature of his conclusions leaves Russell in doubt. If Russell defends anarchist ideas, it is perhaps more because of his distrust of state socialism, of the Marxist variety, than for their inherent appeal. He sees anarchism as 'the ultimate ideal to which society should approximate' rather than an alternative program capable of replacing tomorrow the existing social order.

But he had a solid distrust of state power, well before his 1920 visit to Soviet Russia. For Russell, the critique of capitalism is not solely a criticism of the 'thirst for profit' or a simple revolt against poverty, nor is it based on the inevitability of cyclical crises. It is above all an opposition to the concentration of power engendered by private ownership of the major means of production and the degradation of human life linked to insecurity and merciless competition.

Today, at least in the West, the wretched slums and child labour of the nineteenth century have disappeared, but the lives of thousands of workers can still be ruined by their employers if the latter decide to ship their factories to the other side of the planet. Thus we see that the problem of the power exercised by the owners of the means of production is not solved merely by raising the standard of living.

However, there is no reason to think that the situation would be much better if power were concentrated in the hands of a caste of bureaucrats, thanks to 'socialism', if what that means is the absolute takeover of production and intellectual life by the state. In keeping with the fact that his critique is aimed more against power than against private property as such, Russell displays none of the economic reductionism often found among Marxists, which constantly sees ideological phenomena as the expression of economic relations. For Russell, there is a 'life of instinct' which manifests itself, for example, in nationalism, and is independent of the pursuit of material interests. As he puts it in his critique of Marxism:

> 'To desire one's own economic advancement is comparatively reasonable; to Marx, who inherited eighteenth-century rationalist psychology from the British orthodox economists, self-enrichment seemed the natural aim of a man's political actions. But modern psychology has dived much deeper into the ocean of insanity upon which the little barque of human reason insecurely floats.'1

What is striking nevertheless is the extent to which the theories discussed in this book are close to each other, at least compared to all the rest: communism, fascism, imperialism, neoliberalism – that is, almost everything that really happened after 1918. Moreover, Russell's optimism is astonishing, right in the midst of a war whose end could not be foreseen by anyone in the first months of 1918 (the Russian Revolution had in fact strengthened Germany). His optimism was based on the idea that with the war having shown the failure of the existing system, a new world was going to be built on its ruins. This outlook contrasts sharply with the situation today, when any Left ideas discussed here in France are regarded in general as at best harmless daydreams or, at worst, dangerous utopias.

Finally, the revolution did not take place – at least not the one pre-1914 socialists were thinking of, and no new world emerged from the war. Instead, the First World War gave birth to communism and fascism. Fascination with the former would confuse the radical part of the Left as much as fighting against the latter would absorb all its energy.

Russell, however, remained clear-headed. As early as 1920, he travelled to Soviet Russia to see for himself, and returned without illusions to write *The Practice and Theory of Bolshevism*. Fifty years before the 'revelations' of Solzhenitsyn caused shock and dismay in the French intelligentsia of the 1970s – but also well before Stalin took power, before the Moscow trials and the disillusions of the 1930s, before the writings of Victor Serge and Boris Souvarine – Russell saw what nobody denies today: that the regime put in place by V. I. Lenin and Leon Trotsky in 1917 was a dictatorship, and a ferocious one at that. Above all, he was guided by observation, a critical mind, and common sense. Russell had no grand theory about the social classes in power in Russia, the nature of the Soviet state, or the supposed 'degeneration' of the revolution, such as proliferated among so many Marxist critics of the USSR, particularly among Trotskyists.

Russell observed the mechanisms of the dictatorship rapidly set up after the October Revolution: total suppression of freedom of expression or of assembly for the opposition, even the Left opposition, and creation of a secret police that could act outside the law. As he noted, in the expression 'dictatorship of the proletariat', which on the face of it might indicate an original form of representative government (through the Council system), the word 'dictatorship' is taken literally but not the word 'proletariat'; the latter designated the 'conscious' elements of the proletariat, that is, in practice, the Communists, regardless of their class origin.

It is only fair to stress just how hard it was psychologically, right on the heels of the First World War, to which Russell was so ardently opposed, to be lucid about Soviet Russia, whose revolution had enabled that country to get out of the war. After all, even the Spanish Anarchists joined the Communist International in 1919, 'without hesitation, as a woman gives herself to the man she loves', to echo their expression at the time (they left in 1922).[2] If so many people joined the parties of the Third International, it was precisely because the First World War had convinced them of the total failure of the system that led to it, and they were ready to adhere to whatever radical alternative was available, abandoning all critical sense. In contrast to most of the intellectual Left, Russell always tried not to take his desires for reality.

Russell was also quick to spot what would be a characteristic trait of the Communist movement, namely its 'religious' aspect, often fanatically so. Moreover it is amusing to read today his comparisons of communism and Islam (at the time of its conquests), in light of the fact that the latter has replaced communism in Western demonology. He saw in Lenin an intellectual aristocrat, but one with an extremely dogmatic belief in the doctrines he took to be those of Marx. It was the dogmatic certainty with which the communists defended their doctrines that shocked Russell (and with him all free thinkers) even more than the doctrines themselves.

One cannot overstate the difference between Marx and Lenin. When the latter wanted to 'prove' a point, he tended to cite Marx. Marx didn't cite anyone. Marx was a child of the Enlightenment, authoritarian in some ways and, contrary to the anarchists, not believing in the need to abolish the State immediately after the revolution. But nowhere in Marx is to be

found the idea that socialism can be identified with more or less complete
state control of the economy, much less that the form to be taken by the
socialist State should be a sort of absolute monarchy imposing an official
doctrine in the same way that State religions were imposed in the past.

And yet, despite the evident repulsion that Bolshevism inspired in him,
Russell offers a fairly nuanced vision of the revolution – at least compared
to its critics on the right or on the 'democratic Left'. First, he recognised
that, regarded as a 'splendid attempt', Bolshevism 'deserves the gratitude
and admiration of all the progressive part of mankind'.

Then, when he met the Russian writer Maxim Gorky, Russell said that
if he were Russian, he like Gorky would support the government because
the alternatives were even worse. Russell thought that in seeking to
modernize a backward country, the Bolsheviks were performing 'a
necessary though unamiable task'. He might finally have agreed with the
statement, often attributed to Winston Churchill, that Stalin found a Russia
equipped with a wooden plough and left it in possession of atomic
weapons. His main objection concerns what he called the 'camouflage'
used by the Bolsheviks to claim that their modernising dictatorship was the
ally of socialism such as it was conceived at the time in the West.

Russell's critique of the practice of Bolshevism thus is not aimed
primarily at its action in Russia itself, but rather at the tactics of the
Communist International, especially in the West, and at the idea that
seizing power by an elite made up of 'professional revolutionaries', as
Lenin put it, more or less on the model of what happened in Russia in
1917, was the way to socialism. On that he was completely right, and the
notion of taking power in such a way in developed countries has always
been a myth. While it mobilised some and repulsed others, it was never
anything but a myth.

Where Russell also parted from critics of the Bolshevik Revolution on
the Right or the 'democratic Left' was his view of the Franco-British
entente and the policies towards Russia followed by the imperialist
countries after 1917: an extremely deadly blockade and direct military
interventions. He stressed, and there again history has proved him entirely
right, that those policies by no means weakened Bolshevism, but drove it
to be still more dictatorial, while inflicting dreadful suffering on the
Russian population. As Russell put it, the fact that a man who is deprived
of food and drink will grow weak, go mad, and finally die,

> 'is not usually considered a good reason for inflicting death by starvation. But
> where nations are concerned, the weakness and struggles are regarded as
> morally culpable, and are held to justify further punishment.'

Thus the great powers have used the internal weaknesses of Soviet Russia, and later of China, Vietnam, Iraq, Cuba, or Iran today, to justify more sanctions.

On this point, Russell foresaw what would be the source of one of the major tragedies of the twentieth century: the use, first by European powers and then by the United States, of systematic subversion, direct or indirect assassination, or *coups d'état* to 'kill the hope' aroused by reformist movements and leaders in the Third World: notably Mohammad Mossadegh in Iran, Jacobo Arbenz in Guatemala, Patrice Lumumba in Congo, João Goulart in Brazil, Sukarno in Indonesia, and Salvador Allende in Chile. Moreover, inasmuch as dictatorships are usually harder to overthrow or subvert than democracies, the former are favoured by a sort of unnatural selection. Cuba, for example, has managed more successfully to survive US assaults than democratic reformers such as Arbenz, Goulart or Allende. Iran today is much harder to subvert than it was in Mossadegh's day.

In addition to that unnatural selection, there is a 'barricade effect' which was produced by foreign intervention in the Russian Civil War. When countries are faced with aggression, their tendency is to close in on themselves in self-protection. As an example, it is enough to look at the drastic security measures taken by the US government after September 11, 2001, not to mention its subsequent invasions of Afghanistan and Iraq. Why wouldn't much more sustained assaults provoke similar reactions in other countries? It is impossible to understand the policy of the USSR throughout its history, or of China after 1949, or of Iran today, without taking that effect into account. By the same token, it was having witnessed at first hand the overthrow of Arbenz that radicalised Che Guevara.[3] In 1919, a young Vietnamese came to the Versailles Conference with a proposal to achieve the self-determination of his people. Unceremoniously shown the door, he went to Moscow to complete his political education and went on to make history under the name of Ho Chi Minh.

The 'democratic' Western Left has shown little interest in opposing all those forms of imperialism, with the exception of a few particularly dramatic conflicts, such as the wars in Algeria and Vietnam. But it misses no chance to denounce dictatorship in the Third World today as in the Soviet Union in the past, while completely overlooking the overwhelming responsibility of Western actions in the emergence and radicalisation of those dictatorships. Thus, even when those criticisms are theoretically justified, they are tinged with hypocrisy.

The aspect of Russell's book which remains most timely is,

nevertheless, his critique of the 'theory' of Bolshevism, or the 'materialist theory of history'. Once again, that has very little to do with Marx, even though it is true that Marx had a taste for apodictic formulas giving the impression of a mastery of the laws of historical development. This shows up especially in the *Communist Manifesto* (written when he was twenty-nine years old). And in *Capital* he tried to provide a scientific analysis of how the economy functions, but he was none the less nowhere near the dogmatism of Lenin and his successors.[4]

The 'materialist theory of history' assumes that in the last analysis, human actions are motivated by the desire to possess as much material goods as possible, and that ideological phenomena are to be explained on that basis. In particular, concerning wars such as the one from which the world was barely emerging in 1920, and which Lenin attributed to imperialist rivalry, the dominant idea, not only among Marxists but in the Left in general, was that the working class had been taken in by capitalists who wanted the war in order to increase their profits. This type of explanation is still extremely popular, even among many who have nothing to do with Marxism; most of the current conflicts in the Middle East are explained in terms of oil, while the ideological or religious aspects related to these conflicts are dismissed as the result of ruling-class 'manipulation' of working people.

As Russell stressed, the idea that men act according to rational calculations of how to increase their share of commodities underestimates 'the ocean of insanity upon which the little barque of human reason insecurely floats'. It neglects human passions, the most politically significant being the various forms of religion and nationalism. Citing numerous examples, Russell argued that even if economic factors play an important role, Marxists ignore 'irrational' factors at their peril, and that the notion that wage-earners were dragged into the war because they were 'misled by cunning capitalists' is largely a myth, because the capitalists were 'in the grip of nationalist instinct as much as their proletarian "dupes".'

Russell observed the human tendency to rationalise conduct that is in reality motivated by drives and sentiments. In war, there are two ways to go about this: the 'idealist' will claim to fight for democracy, and the 'materialist' will claim to defend his economic interests. Marxists, observed Russell, see through the idealistic 'camouflage', but not through the other.

Of course, Russell never denied that every war is accompanied by enormous propaganda in its favour, but he notes that there are some things that even the most intense propaganda fails to accomplish: for example, to make Irish Catholics into Englishmen, and more generally to manage to alter the sentimental attachments that bind a human group to its identity, religion or nation. These attachments are due to human psychology and are inexplicable in terms of profit-seeking or manipulation by the ruling class.

In fact, these irrational but profoundly human factors, much more than the action of the ruling classes themselves, are probably what have historically constituted the greatest obstacle to achieving socialism. Much of Russell's reflection, in common with most pacifists, has been the attempt to find ways, such as appropriate education and systematic criticism of irrationality, to control self-destructive human passions. It is sometimes comical to observe how 'Marxists' dismiss such efforts as a waste of time, since in their view ideological phenomena will solve themselves once 'the revolution' has transferred the means of production to the state.

The most damaging intellectual confusion of the Twentieth Century has no doubt been to identify socialism with the Soviet adventure. The Soviet Union was the result of a tragic and violent history: civil War and foreign interventions, the need to modernise and defend the nation from Nazi invasion, and unimaginable sacrifices accomplished in order to win the Second World War. None of that was foreseen or foreseeable before 1914, and surely not even the 'statist' socialists of that period hoped for the type of absolute dictatorship that emerged from those hardships. That identification nevertheless was made, both by the enemies of socialism, who sought thereby to discredit it, and by the communists who sought by the same identification to embellish the image of the Soviet Union.

One could have hoped that with the collapse of the Soviet Union, that confusion would be cleared up, but it is the very opposite that took place. Even those who maintained that the USSR was not 'genuine socialism' (an expression which presumes that another socialism is possible) for the most part declared, after 1991, that socialism itself was a failure. The European social democratic parties adopted privatisation policies that were the exact opposite of what they had advocated at the time when the USSR still existed.

And this raises the question as to who was right in the end, Russell or Lenin and the Bolsheviks. The fall of the Soviet Union, as well as the horrors accompanying its history, seem to answer unambiguously in favour of Russell. But things are not so simple, because the fall of the Soviet Union by no means marked a triumph of Russell's ideas. There is no doubt that Russell was one of the first socialists to keep reminding those 'who were dazzled by the external success of the Soviet Union, that they had forgotten the painful lessons of absolute monarchy,' that is, the corrupting effects of absolute power.[5] He also refused to engage in one-sided criticism ignoring history and the domestic and foreign obstacles weighing on the Russian Revolution, that would merely have played into the hands of imperialists and reactionaries. By adopting a subtle and nuanced attitude, he pleased no one, neither the communists nor the anti-communists.

Today, alongside all the negative aspects, which are sufficiently known to everyone, the positive achievements of the communist movement should not be ignored: the victory over fascism, obviously, but also its significant contribution to the major emancipation of the twentieth century, namely the colonial liberation movement. It is actually more realistic to see the communist movement outside Western Europe as part of the global revolt against imperialism (Russell also points to that essential aspect in Lenin's speeches) than as a contribution to socialism.

In Western Europe, despite its revolutionary rhetoric, the communist movement has in practice more or less amounted to a branch of social democracy, which after the Second World War made great strides in terms of public services, social security, and democratic education. In his own country, Britain, the moment when ideas close to those of Russell were most put into practice was doubtless following the victory of the Labour Party in 1945.[6] But, even there, it is questionable whether those transformations would have been possible without the victory of the Soviet Union in the war, without the inspiration it provided (rightly or wrongly) to the workers, and the fear it aroused in the ruling classes. An answer to that question is perhaps provided by the fact that, after 1991, far from seeing the rise of a radical 'non-Stalinist' Left, such a Left has completely vanished, as social democracy has become neoliberal and the Left intelligentsia has turned to the joys of postmodernism and identity politics, while European green movements have abandoned their pacifism to support 'humanitarian wars'.

To return to the comparison between Lenin and Russell, one may ask what status, what effectiveness a free intellectual, independent of any party, can possibly have in the arena of political conflicts. Communism was a mass movement bringing together tens of millions of people, whereas Russell was an intellectual, no doubt as influential as an intellectual can be, but with no mass movement behind him. Even today, in the whole world there are surely more members of the international communist movement than people who have even heard of Russell.

Incidentally, without Lenin, the name of Marx himself might well have ended up in the same category, since most of the socialist movement was moving away from his ideas in the early years of the twentieth century (leaving aside the question as to what extent Lenin really propagated the ideas of Marx, rather than a considerably distorted version).

Political conflicts tend to be dominated precisely by those irrational passions whose very existence is denied or played down by Marxism. All too often the violence of the oppressors, fascists, imperialists, or colonialists can be combated effectively only by the violence of the oppressed, and the voice of reason is drowned out in the tumult of battle. Of what use can it be?

It was perhaps in response to that objection that Russell maintained that the four most powerful men in history were the Buddha, Jesus Christ, Pythagoras, and Galileo, none of whom enjoyed official support in their lifetime nor disposed of any power other than that of persuasion.[7] The underlying idea being that the force of arms carries the day in the short term, but in the long term ideas win out. In their lifetime, Lenin, Stalin, and Mao enjoyed enormous popularity, which eroded sharply once they were gone. The emancipating ideas contained in the best of classic liberalism, in the defence of rationalism, pacifism, and a truly libertarian education, continue to spread. Russell's liberal ideas have enjoyed considerable success. His book on *Marriage and Morals* could be shocking in 1929, but seems quite banal today, as do his critique of religion and his anti-militarism. But the prospect of socialisation of the means of production within a democratic framework, which was also one of his fundamental aspirations, seems more remote than ever.

Russell was both a liberal and a socialist, a combination that was perfectly comprehensible in his time, but which has become almost unthinkable today. He was a liberal in that he opposed concentrations of power in all its manifestations, military, governmental, or religious, as well as the superstitious or nationalist ideas that usually serve as its justification. But he was also a socialist, even as an extension of his liberalism, because he was equally opposed to the concentrations of power stemming from the private ownership of the major means of production, which therefore needed to be put under social control (which does not mean state control).

But there was a major lacuna in the socialist vision of the world before 1914, concerning what were then called the 'barbarians', that is the world outside the West. If Russell can be criticised for his terminology, which was that of his era, he was far ahead of others in adopting an anti-imperialist attitude and commented ironically on the colonial exploitation that a socialist government would perpetuate.

For the major social transformation of the twentieth century was not in the direction of socialism but rather was decolonisation (the communist movement in Asia should be seen primarily as anti-colonial and anti-feudal, its adhesion to 'communism' being essentially a means of gaining international support). That transformation has had a profound impact on Western socialism. Already in 1902, the English writer J A Hobson (whose celebrity is partly due to the fact that his work served as the basis of Lenin's *Imperialism, the Highest Stage of Capitalism*) saw that the opportunities for Western capitalists to invest in the colonies would create a situation in which 'little clusters of wealthy aristocrats' would draw 'dividends and pensions from the Far East' and would thus support, thanks to this tribute,

> 'great tame masses of retainers, no longer engaged in the staple industries of agriculture and manufacture, but kept in the performance of personal or minor industrial services under the control of a new financial aristocracy.' Hobson warned that this situation, 'far from forwarding the cause of world-civilisation, might introduce the gigantic peril of a Western parasitism.'[8]

Just how much Hobson's predictions have come true is evident from a *New York Times* report of how Apple got an urgent job done. Although it was the middle of the night, a foreman aroused eight thousand Chinese workers in the company's dormitories, gave each a biscuit and a cup of tea, put them to work for a solid twelve-hour shift, and within ninety-six hours, the plant was producing over ten thousand iPhones a day.[9]

Another way to look at the problem posed by the existence of the world outside the West is to imagine that the developed countries have always been totally isolated from the rest of the world: no cheap raw materials, no immigrant work force, no goods produced under the conditions just described. It is obvious that our society would be completely different from what it is: the level of consumption would be much lower, but we would also have to produce what we consume, which would create a relationship of forces quite different between workers and employers.

We can only speculate on the type of society such a situation would create, but it might very well resemble the socialism that was dreamed of before 1914. Of course, the point here is not to blame the rest of the world for the present situation, but to emphasise that what has enabled the existing system to survive is in large part the existence of a hinterland, former colonies that became the Third World and then emerging nations, on which we shifted many of our problems. But that observation leads to two conclusions concerning socialism. First of all, far from having disappeared, the working class is still in formation on the world scale: in Asia and in Latin America, the transformation of peasants into workers is under way, while in Africa it is only beginning. No one knows how these upheavals will end. As for the developed countries, their hegemony over the rest of the world is in constant decline; if the day comes when these countries are obliged to solve their own problems without being able to shift them abroad, the question of another form of social organisation will arise once more.

Moreover, everything that is more or less civilised in the developed countries – social security, democratic education, protection of workers, public services – was created in an essentially socialist spirit. In economic terms, a good part of life – childhood, youth, old age, illness, unemployment – is already socialised. True, the neoliberal offensive aims to dismantle those achievements, but it is running up against a disorganised but obstinate resistance, because those achievements are still very popular.

In *The Spirit Level*, Richard Wilkinson and Kate Pickett show statistically that in the Western world, relatively egalitarian societies (thanks to partial application of socialist ideas) enjoy enormous advantages in terms of health, safety, education, social mobility, and so on.[10] In *America Beyond Capitalism*, Gar Alperovitz reviews all the more or less collective enterprises that already exist even in the 'capitalist paradise' of the United States.[11] In Spain the Mondragon co-operative, with its 35,000 employees, demonstrates that economic democracy and efficiency are not necessarily contradictory.

Of course, none of that is perfect and in many ways remains marginal. But at least it shows that the ideas of classical socialism are not dead. In a period when the main forces opposing each other in the Western world are, on one hand, a democratic 'Left' and Right both converted to neoliberalism and, on the other, various reactionary currents, the ideas of Russell can help to keep afloat the fragile barque of human reason and offer the prospect, however distant, of a truly human world.

Notes

1 Bertrand Russell, (London: George Allen and Unwin,1920; Nottingham: Spokesman, 1995)

2 Daniel Guérin, (Paris: Gallimard, 1965),132–36.

3 Che was to write later: 'I was in Guatemala at the time, the Guatemala of

Arbenz, and I began to draft some notes for rules of revolutionary medicine. I began to think about what was needed to be a revolutionary doctor. But then came the aggression, the aggression let loose by United Fruit, the State Department, Foster Dulles – anyway, all that in reality is the same thing – and the puppet they set up was called Castillo Armas ... I then realised something essential: that to be revolutionary doctor, or simply to be a revolutionary, what is needed first of all is for there to be a revolution. Isolated individual effort, pure ideals, the desire to sacrifice a whole life to the noblest ideals, all that is useless if one is acting by oneself alone in some remote corner of America, struggling against hostile governments and social conditions that block all progress.' (',' speech given in Havana on August 19, 1960, available at http://cubanismo.net).

4 According to Engels' biographer, Tristram Hunt, the 'materialist concept of history' owes more to Engels than to Marx.
5 Bertrand Russell, 'Why I Am Not a Communist', in (Nottingham, UK: Spokesman, 1995), 213.
6 See Ken Loach's 2013 documentary film , to appreciate the achievements and mentality of that period.
7 Bertrand Russell, (London: George Allen and Unwin, 1938).
8 John Atkinson Hobson, (Nottingham, UK: Spokesman, 2011).
9 Charles Duhigg and Keith Bradsher, 'How the U.S. Lost Out on iPhone Work', January 21, 2012.
10 Richard Wilkinson and Kate Pickett, (London: Penguin, 2010).
11 Gar Alperovitz, second ed. (Takoma Park, MD: Democracy Collaborative, 2011).

www.monthlyreview.org

'Socialism, like everything else that is vital, is rather a tendency than a strictly definable body of doctrine.'
Bertrand Russell, Roads to Freedom

Reviews

Jeremy

Alex Nunns, *The Candidate: Jeremy Corbyn's Improbable Path to Power*, OR Books, 2016, 406 pages, ISBN 9781682190647, £15

There have been only a handful of books that I have felt it necessary to read. There are several I have wanted to read. And then there are books that you are sceptical will tell a truthful account of events you personally recall, or of circumstances in which you had some small part to play, but you feel you need to read them anyway.

I was on the outermost reaches of the unfolding events in *The Candidate: Jeremy Corbyn's Improbable Path to Power*. I was entirely sceptical that there would be an even-handed and impartial recounting of even some of the events that I could recall. In that climate of suspicion, I began to read. I have to say that it was most engaging, purely on the conversational yet detailed and informed style of writing. Unlike my expectation of a slanted and wholly 'broadsheet media' treatment of the subject matter, the author offered a cogent and coherent explanation of the unlikely events. Some of his interviews were quoted, and other aspects of interviews just referenced. Nonetheless, what was most refreshing and disarming was the ability of the interviewer (the author) to represent in a wholly impartial manner the even more refreshingly honest appraisals and answers provided by the interviewees. There was no dressing up or mitigations in the presentation of what was this wholly absorbing read, which I surprisingly started and finished during the afternoon and evening of the day of receipt.

The warts-and-all exposé of the unlikeliest transition of Jeremy Corbyn, from the outer edges of the left of the Labour Party into the reluctantly-accepted position of candidate for leader, proved to be deeply insightful. Whereas with the TV docudrama *Theresa v Boris*, about the election battle for the leadership of the Conservative party, not one of the candidates or participant parties acquitted themselves well, or even came across as remotely approachable (let alone likeable!) or honest. The complete opposite is, for me, true of the main protagonists in The *Candidate*. Whilst they do present themselves as being deeply serious and thoughtful politicians they are nonetheless absolutely realistic about their initial ambitions and their reasoning for their actions. It was fascinating to see how they coped and rationalised each changing position as the horizon of expectation kept on moving forward rather than stopping, as they expected, and waiting for them to walk into it, stumble and fall away. As a retired trade unionist it reminds me of – and has many parallels to – the succession to power of my own General Secretary, Mark Serwotka (Public and Commercial Services Union), whose own leadership began with an equally dedicated and committed group of trade union socialists determining that a candidate from the left should at least stand in the leadership election. Mark's success was a testament to those dedicated individuals and the campaign they fought. Jeremy Corbyn also took some time to volunteer to be the 'point man', with low expectations for success, and even less ambition to be Labour Party leader.

The Labour Party leadership election campaign is not what I would normally be recommending to people to read about, unless they were deeply political and invested in campaigning. However, this book reads more like a real-life thriller. I could readily identify with many of the actions of other citizens who also felt it was time for change. Fortunately, they had the drive and determination to not let this opportunity pass them by, and to attempt to give their best and communicate the importance of not missing this moment and opportunity for change. Their actions thrilled, excited, and shamed me in equal measure. As a trade unionist, I felt that I should have done much more than merely advocate to members, write emails, and forward mails and twitter links.

Regardless of my guilt, the book makes clear how transformative was the campaign, and innovative in the manner of its application. When being educated about the Industrial Revolution, my teacher provided us with a quote: 'necessity is the mother of invention'. Well, some of the campaigners from the general public were accepted as contributors by the inner circle of the Corbyn team, and those few inner circle people showed how openness and independent thinking can offer a huge benefit; let's hope not just for this campaign, but for future conduct in both politics and wider society. *The Candidate* shows how, from improbable beginnings and with limited expectations, given the right attitudes of those running the campaign, hope can transform even the most limited of expectations into a truly innovative and positive campaigning movement. That is not to say that you can just step up with an idea and it will catch a mood. Corbyn and McDonnell have been ploughing their political ideas in this particular left field for over 30 years, so the actual seeds of this most unexpected of events were sown very deep before even a leaflet was drawn.

This is a highly engaging book whose central figure is, by turns, diffident, humble, and yet determined. Indeed, no different to the public persona. A very different read about a very different politician. I found it literally unputdownable. Now it's your turn.

Dave Putson

Alice Bacon MP

Rachel Reeves with Richard Carr, *Alice in Westminster: The Political Life of Alice Bacon*, I.B.Tauris, 2017, 240 pages, hardback ISBN 9781784537685, £20

'I hope you will enjoy your short stay in Westminster' – ungracious 1945 Tory congratulation. Bacon would remain there until 1970, retiring undefeated. 'All but unknown' – Alex Smallwood, *TLS* 24 February 2017. Reeves herself admits she only heard of Bacon 'about six years ago'. 'A challenge to biographers' (Smallwood). Alice, to her credit, never published self-promoting diaries or autobiography.

Reeves (evidenced in her 5-page bibliography, plus YouTube interview) brought home the Bacon via archival documents, mentions in other politico-diaries (e.g. Castle, Crossman), and conversations with former MPs (especially Gerald Kaufman) and veteran Leeds Labourites who knew her. She might have mentioned that Bacon's 3,584 Commons speeches are available on the Hansard website; also various newspaper obituaries (online).

Appropriate that Bacon is resuscitated in this widely-acclaimed biography by her direct successor as female Leeds Labour MP. One immediate fruit was the 'Alice Bacon Event' hosted (21 April 2017) by Yvette Cooper. Less fitting that co-author Richard Carr's name does not share cover-billing.

Reeves' introduction sets the tone, adumbrating Bacon's lifelong socialism and her legislative/personal priorities. Earliest encouragement came from her miner father. One naturally compares the Grantham grocer's daughter. Bacon detested Thatcher, hence noteworthy that the latter (1966 interview) hailed Bacon as female pioneer on becoming first-ever woman minister of state (Home Office). Not that Bacon was a modern-style feminist, indeed frequently disavowing the label, echoing Barbara Castle's 'I am no feminist. Judge me only as a socialist' in her victory speech: 'we were not elected because we are women, but because we are Labour candidates believing in a socialist cause'.

Bacon inevitably suffered from male condescension, then common in all parties. Reeves quotes some trenchant remarks of Lena Jeger MP - Herbert Morrison told her 'stick to women's problems' – leading Bacon (supported by Castle) to establish separate Labour female cadres, prefiguring modern quotas.

Bacon also suffered from now unthinkable personal insults about her 'grating' ('unbearable', Crossman) voice and 'plump homely figure' – in several of the 23 illustrations, she is actually quite fetching. Not that Bacon was herself entirely innocent, joking about Bessie Braddock's rotundity. Nor was her image improved when her knickers once fell down in mid-Commons speech.

Bacon's lifelong spinsterhood did not help. Close friend Denis Healey dubbed her 'a Jane Eyre [she did two pre-parliamentary teaching stints – despite supposed opposition to corporal punishment, pupils remembered her as a caner] who never found her Mr Rochester'. Some (e.g. Shirley Williams) speculated she might have found one in her idol, Hugh Gaitskell. Reeves' disbelief is probably right. She might have mentioned his Lotharian career. As a WEA lecturer in 1920s Nottingham, Gaitskell lived 'under the brush' with a local woman, dismissing marriage as 'bourgeois convention'. Later, he conducted a flagrant liaison with Ian Fleming's wife, Ann. Impressive record for the man Nye Bevan dismissed as 'a desiccated calculating machine'.

Healey also christened Bacon 'Terror of the Trotskyites' for expelling Cliff and Barbara Slaughter, luminaries of that other Healy's Socialist Labour League. Her antipathy to the far left went back to the anti-Red campaign (1929) of miners' leader A. J. Cook against communist infiltration. Her *Times* obituary recalled her 'smoking out heresy and recommending expulsions'. Trotskyite blood pressures would also have shot up over her unexpected kind words for Stalin, whom (1944) she met in Russia.

Reeves charts Bacon's course throughout the turbulent 1960s, both deploring and provoking the Left-Right splits and the Party's losing its working-class roots – very prophetic. After Gaitskell's sudden death (cp. John Smith's, later), there rose Harold Wilson, with whom Bacon and some others formed a 'Yorkshire Mafia'. Reeves largely ignores the Clause IV controversy and the ups-and-downs of nationalisation overall, though quoting Wilson's quip that revising it would be 'akin to taking Genesis out of the Bible'. Here also, an otherwise excellent account of Bacon and the Co-operative Party might have mentioned its admirable Sunday paper, *Reynold's News*, sadly long defunct.

As Minister of State, Bacon was much involved in the great social liberalisings that (inter alia) decriminalised homosexuality and abortion, saw capital punishment abolished, and the 1968 Race Relations Act –

Crossman called her 'magnificent' in support. This last inevitably recalls Powell's 'rivers of blood' speech, though one should also remember some Alf Garnett-like dockers marching in 'Enoch's' support, and the Sheffield Labour MP who, post-*Windrush,* immediately called for immigration caps and the right of dance halls to debar 'coloureds'. Nor can Reeves herself claim any moral high ground, given her 2016 description of Leeds West as 'like a tinderbox that could explode if immigration was not curbed'. Shades, here, of this couplet from an old Rupert Bear story:

> '*Cries Reggie Rabbit in dismay/Weird foreigners are on the way.*'

For sharp insight into the cultural and emotional impact of black immigration, Colin McInnes' trilogy of novels (*Absolute Beginners, City of Spades, Mr Love & Justice*) cannot be bettered.

'Woy' Jenkins is automatically identified with these changes, thanks not least to his hyper-egotistical memoir *Roy: A Life at the Centre* (1991). Reeves convincingly discloses the credit due to Bacon and Leo Abse. 'Woy' was reputedly lazy, inspiring Nye Bevan to remark:

> 'Anyone who worked so hard at his accent could not be described in such terms.'

Likewise, there was Bacon's role in the drive for comprehensive education and the belittlement of grammar schools. Everyone remembers Anthony Crosland's infamous promise 'to destroy every fucking grammar school'. But, Bacon (reshuffled to Education, 1967), for whom this was her 'ideological rather than practical' passion (Reeves, p.157) was the battering ram. Chapter 5 is entirely devoted to this, with much gloating over Thatcher's inability to stem the tide, Reeves calling it Bacon's 'greatest personal and political legacy'.

Not for me, a working-class boy who owes everything to his Lincoln School (1948-56) teachers. Reeves' claim (p.161) that 'the 11+ exam was skewed towards benefiting middle-class children' is simply not true. In response to Bacon (herself grammar school), Crosland, and company, I always invoke the passionate defence of grammar schools by Attlee's Minister of Education, 'Red' Ellen Wilkinson. Contrariwise, Neil Kinnock protested to the BBC over a 'one-sided' *Archers* episode in which Shula defended the Borchester Grammar School, demanding equal time for the Comprehensive argument – he didn't get it.

Whilst fighting these battles, Bacon never neglected her constituents, praised for her 'surgeries', in contrast to the absentee MPs (mainly Tory) castigated by Thatcherite Ferdinand Mount.

Bacon's odder side comes out in her Leavis-like hostility to 'popular culture', not only denigrating The Beatles and Rolling Stones, but objecting to the television screening of British crime drama *The Blue Lamp* – perhaps the shooting of Dixon of Dock Green was too much for her?

After an envoi remarking Bacon's last triumph (unmasking John Poulson), her uneasy but effective Lords speeches, the long, enigmatic friendship (possibly more?) with journalist Eric Stacpoole (one of very few trusted by Wilson), before rapid health decline, leading to death from broncho-pneumonia, 24 March, 1993, Reeves leaves the last words to long-time colleague Bernard Atha:

'Alice was like a rock for the Labour Party ... there was no messing with Alice.'

Buttressed by terse, referential end-notes, five statistical appendixes, and a just-about-adequate index, this is a timely book for the Labour Party – a sense of déja vu frequently pervades. Although written in undistinguished (though commendably jargon-free), sometimes plodding, prose, Reeves and Carr have given us a welcome, long-overdue tribute to a woman who was both ordinary and extraordinary.

Barry Baldwin

Vietnam revisited

Tom Hayden, *Hell No: The Forgotten Power of the Vietnam Peace Movement,* Yale University Press, 2017, 160 pages, hardback ISBN 9780300218671

John Marciano, *The American War in Vietnam: Crime or Commemoration?* Monthly Review Press, New York, 2016, 196 pages, paperback ISBN 9781583675854, hardback ISBN 9781583675861

These are two very different books but they cover much the same ground. The protest movement against the Vietnam War is being slowly airbrushed out of history. It is not always the winners who write the histories; the losers can do a pretty good job, too.

Tom Hayden, who died late last year, is hardly a household name in the UK and indeed one wonders if he is remembered even in the USA today. If he is remembered at all, it is for his marriage to Jane Fonda, another very committed and active resister of the war. But he was a big name in the sixties: he was one of the founders of SDS (Students for a Democratic

Society) and one of the Chicago 8, who were tried for conspiracy. The eight represented the gamut of the Protest-Resistance Movement: from Dave Dellinger, an old hand who had been involved his whole life, Rennie Davis, the more buttoned-up, 'straight' politico, to Bobby Seale, the only Afro-American defendant, bound in chains on the orders of Judge Julius Hoffman – who makes the judge at Jeremy Thorpe's trial the picture of benign partiality – and so on to the Yippies, Jerry Rubin and Abbie Hoffman. (Yippies, not Hippies: they believed in Flower Power well enough but were convinced that drugs, sex and rock 'n' roll could be combined with a dedicated commitment to political action, and proved that it could.)

So, understandably, Tom Hayden's emphasis is on the movement on campus, but he recognises and pays tribute to the Veterans for Peace and the various Afro-American groups.

John Marciano's work has a broader sweep; it's a more general history and very interesting, too, but poorly edited with much repetition. Marciano scoffs at the idea that the Peace Movement started with the Vietnam War. After the Second World War, American troops were mightily pissed off when their troopships, that were supposed to take them back home, were used to take French troops to Vietnam so they could join fully-armed Japanese troops in attempting to crush the Vietnamese independence movement.

Still, there can be no doubt the anti-war movement reached extraordinary proportions during the Vietnam War. From my own experience, there wasn't such a split between campus and veteran groups. I was never a member of any special grouping, but there was always a mixture of students and veterans who weren't students. Indeed, I was glad of the vets' presence; they beefed up our nerdy image and gave us some credibility in the face of some very outraged and hostile audiences. The mothers of 'our boys in Nam' were the most terrifying – I was grateful for the presence of police at times, even though once involved in a massive police riot in Washington.

Whites and blacks didn't mix much, although Martin Luther King had a huge white following. He is, himself, one of the victims of airbrushing both authors are so determined to combat. His 'I Have a Dream' speech is deservedly well known, but little is heard of his Riverside Church speech in which he denounced the war in Vietnam and called the US Government 'the greatest purveyor of violence in the world'. Who has heard *of* it, never mind actually heard it? But then American elites have always been good at airbrushing: slavery was a sad mistake (not a criminal system) and hell! – we have had a black president so everything is all right then. And the

Revolutionary War (The War of Independence) which was, in reality, the First American Civil War, has been so mythologized as to have little or nothing to do with what actually happened. Indigenous Indians, while no longer redskin devils, remain practically invisible and the recent controversy of the oil pipeline nearby the Standing Rock Reservation follows the old dismal pattern: we need your land, we want your gold, we want your oil, so don't mess with our superior, civilised ways.

Of course, not even American elites could deny that the Vietnam War was a catastrophe, but only because the US lost, not because it was wrong or criminal, as both authors claim. It was a sad mistake: poor Uncle Sam was only trying to stand up for what he has always believed: Democracy, Freedom, 'our way of life', 'our values', 'the Free World'. Ask Indonesia, Latin America, the Caribbean, and most Middle East countries, not to speak of Cambodia and Laos, how they feel. And the My Lai Massacre was a one-off 'mistake', not, as John Marciano claims, part of a regular pattern. So, Americans feel very sorry for themselves, and there are plenty of films to justify that: *The Deer Hunter*, *Full Metal Jacket*, *Apocalypse Now*, *Platoon*, and the unspeakable *Green Berets*. Our poor boys in Vietnam went through hell. I am sure they did and you can feel sorry for them just as you can for those poor German boys on the Eastern Front in World War Two. But why were they there in the first place, and what about the 'enemy', which, in both cases, included millions of civilians? In American history you hear very little of this. In the films, you hardly see the Vietnamese at all. When you do, they are usually torturers, real bad guys, or whores offering off-duty grunts 'nice fucky-fucky, good time'. You would never know three countries were devastated and that hundreds of thousands died and that chemical weapons were used with abandon, the long-term effects of which are still with the peoples of South East Asia.

It would seem that the subtitle of Tom Hayden's book, 'The Forgotten Power of the Vietnam Peace Movement', is something of a misnomer. If it had been more powerful, it wouldn't have been forgotten. He quotes Thomas Powers' 1973 study *Vietnam: The War at Home*:

> 'The anti-war movement in the United States created the necessary conditions for the shift in official policy from escalation to disengagement.'

John Marciano would agree with this verdict, but I am not sure I do. I left the USA in 1970. The war still had another five years to run. The spies, agents provocateurs, underground agents, disinformation that penetrated the Peace Movement had considerable success.

It must be hard for activists like Tom Hayden or writer/activists such as

Noam Chomsky, Howard Zinn, Naomi Klein or David Noble, who have spent lifetimes fighting the good fight, to have had so little success (which is not to say they shouldn't have fought). 'No more Vietnams' was the slogan, and what have we got? Permanent war. And Noam Chomsky saying the Occupy movement could be the dawn to a new world, and urging his many (but not enough) admirers to vote for the dreadful Hillary to keep out the ghastly Donald.

If you are interested in those times, and in American foreign policy of the day, or in any way participated in the events, then these two books might well appeal. But things have moved on, and have probably got worse.

Nigel Potter

'Bollocks really'

Tom Mills, *The BBC: The Myth of Public Service*, Verso, 2016, 272 pages, hardback ISBN 9781784829, £13.59, ebook 9781784850, £8.99

This book confirms many of the criticisms of the BBC made by the left, and lays bare the close relationship between higher management of that institution and what C. Wright Mills called the 'power elite'. Government, of course, has the ultimate financial sanction through the licence fee, and Mills' text takes us through the history of these control mechanisms and the changes in management priorities and style. Remarkably, is estimated that 'one in sixteen adults' around the world use BBC News Services. Such a broad sweep of listeners and viewers obviously means a great deal of power and influence, and is therefore always inherently too tempting a vehicle for government to leave undisturbed.

The author is adamant that the BBC 'has never been independent of the state in any meaningful sense'. From its very inception the BBC was there to influence the multitudes to look upon the actions of government positively, particularly at times of national crisis. It also acts in times of crisis as the public mouthpiece of the government. In 1926 during the General Strike, the BBC demonstrated its influence to aid the power of government. With all national newspapers hit by the strike, the BBC was virtually the only source of national news and was quickly enlisted as a propaganda aid to the government. This power to influence was immediately recognised by the first General Manager and later Director-General of the BBC, John Reith, who pursued a struggle for a modicum of independence against those such as Winston Churchill who sought to make it a 'state broadcaster'. At the time of the General Strike, Churchill was Chancellor of the Exchequer and a vicious opponent of the striking workers, both as editor of the *British Gazette* and in Cabinet, advocating the use of armed force. Mills goes into considerable detail over the arguments within the BBC and government at the time. It is at this point that the veneer of 'political neutrality', 'balance', 'independence' and 'impartiality' was to be outwardly trumpeted, whilst it got on with the business of 'collector and distributor of Government news, censored where necessary but undoctored'. The latter statement came from the pen of the government's public relations head entrusted with liaison between the BBC and Reith.

The establishment of elite control, whilst still licensing operational independence, is coupled with the overall integration of the upper echelons of the BBC into the web of governmental and financial power through its overtly independent status as a Corporation, granted by Royal Charter, and by the commonality of the recruits to that level. Unarguably, the BBC is run by government appointed trustees who carefully choose the personnel for the higher managerial posts – so carefully, in fact, that *The Social Mobility and Child Poverty Commission*, chaired by such establishment luminaries as Alan Milburn and Baroness Gillian Shephard, when it investigated the BBC, had no difficulty in characterising its management as members of 'Britain's elite'. Not surprisingly, even if the applicants were all Oxbridge graduates, this was not in itself a passport to a position with the BBC. There existed a secret vetting procedure to weed out those whose politics might be questionable, rather than Soviet agents. Sir Hugh Carlton Greene, one of the most culturally liberal of the Director-Generals, was very keen on the procedure as, for him, it served to make for editorial impartiality or, as some would say, conformity throughout the editorial process.

The second chapter, entitled 'The BBC and the Secret State', constitutes an exhaustive study, tracing the development of the relationship of the BBC with the various intelligence agencies. Formally, it began on 21 December 1933 – the BBC Controller of Programmes, an old Etonian, Colonel Alan Dawnay, (formally of the War Office) was to meet with MI5's Brigadier Oswald 'Jasper' Harker, head of counter subversion and espionage. Over a no doubt highly civilised lunch, these two servants of the state met to set up the rudimentary controls that would ensure that (in Harker's words) no 'subversive propaganda' or 'undesirable persons' besmirched the BBC's good name.

The BBC: The Myth of Public Service goes on to describe in some detail the setting up of a system of vetting of potential employees that presumably sought to avoid heavy-footed editorial intervention at a later stage. The author thinks this was the first official meeting between the BBC and the security services, and this harmonious co-operation resulted in vetting the likes of Hugh Dalton, a former Labour Minister, the economist J.A. Hobson, J.L. Stocks for his association with an anti-fascist relief organisation, and John McMurray for speaking at anti-war gatherings. Poetry readings on air by C.S. Lewis and W.H. Auden caused particular perturbation in the BBC's corridors of power. Mills goes on to describe the expansion of the BBC's relationship with the 'secret state' during World War Two, the Cold War, and now the 'war on terror'.

In the distant past, the BBC was controlled by the Post Office and then by the Foreign Office and, given its major propaganda role in wartime, ended up during World War Two under the remit of the Ministry of Information. Reith himself was made Minister of Information for a few months in 1940, and the importance of the BBC to government when Britain is at war can hardly be exaggerated. BBC reportage of the Falklands/Malvinas conflict, the Suez debacle, and the first Iraq war were crucial in making many British people fall into line. In particular, coverage of the Falklands War was a gift to Thatcher's nationalist 1983 election campaign.

A most tumultuous recent war-reporting imbroglio involving the BBC was that concerning the weapons expert, Dr. David Kelly, the 'Dodgy Dossier' on Iraq, and then BBC reporter Andrew Gilligan. Dr. Kelly was found dead in mysterious circumstances and Gilligan's broadcast concerning the 'sexed up . . . Dossier' led to the resignations of Greg Dyke (Director-General) and Gavin Davies (Chairman). These events were used by some in the media to argue that the BBC had taken a stance of independent interrogation of UK participation in the Iraq invasion. For Tom Mills this is not the case at all: for him the abject apology, the resignation of the two senior directors, and the promise to tighten editorial vetting smacked not of fearless independence but craven acquiescence.

Other important matters touched upon include treatment of trade unions, specifically mentioning bias the BBC showed during the year long miners' strike and the anti-trade union, pro-business manipulation of economic reporting. There is a long piece on the myth of BBC leftist bias, carefully cultivated by a Tory coterie of MPs and hack servants in the press, which coincides with the demise of those newspapers having a semblance of objectivity concerning the travails of the labour movement. The *News Chronicle*'s absorption by the *Daily Mail* and the metamorphosis of the *Daily Herald* into Murdoch's *The Sun* represent perhaps the most notable examples of the rise of the 'Red Tops' and the denigration of the BBC as a leftist redoubt. Mills details the history of the so-called BBC leftist deviation through the fabrications of Mary Whitehouse, Norman Tebbit, Brian Crosier, Enoch Powell, Julian Lewis and Boris Johnson. Perhaps the most pertinent quote is from an ex-BBC presenter, one Robert Peston, describing the idea of left-wing bias at the BBC as 'bollocks really'.

The BBC: The Myth of Public Service also contains the history of how the neo-liberal rot set in when Keith Joseph took up the matter of a documentary by the world-renowned Keynesian economist, J.K. Galbraith. With the monetarists now ascendant in Thatcher's Cabinet, the Iron Lady herself took a swipe at the BBC for disseminating the wrong doctrine. Thatcher, with the agreement of Tebbit and Rupert Murdoch, appointed Marmaduke Hussey as a BBC executive. The liberal-leaning Alasdair Milne was 'summarily' dismissed, to be replaced at the helm by Michael Checkland, but the Board insisted Checkland have a deputy, John Birt. The latter installed a marketised structure, centralised decision-making, and the outsourcing of a lot more actual production to commercial companies.

Throughout its history, the BBC has indulged itself with public presenters penning peons to its own democratic credentials and its efforts to bind the nation together and support parliamentary democracy. However, there were at times, and still are, brief interludes of acceptable openness, but the pressure to keep up with the bread and circuses (or should that be cookery and sport?) of other channels seems at times overwhelming. For Tom Mills, reform of the BBC would entail hiring senior staff, freed from establishment control, and the whole institution subjected to 'a more democratic system of public accountability'. Alternative social media activity helped mightily to redress the vile avalanche of hostile propaganda from the mainstream media aimed at Corbyn during the 2017 General Election. What would have been the result if BBC broadcasting had been truly representative of civil society, instead of wallowing in its self-defined 'impartiality' − a left Labour government?

John Daniels

Recto and Verso

Vladimir Mayakovsky, *'Vladimir Mayakovsky' & Other Poems*, translated and edited by James Womack, Fyfield Books/Carcanet Press, 2016, 240 pages, paperback ISBN 9781784102920

This is a gorgeous book. The reader will find it either a seductive introduction or a thrilling reunion. James Womack's translations are bristling with appropriate vigour. The epitome of the revolutionary poet, out on the streets, swift to respond to events, yelling his texts to the crowd, Vladimir Mayakovsky was also a playwright, actor and graphic artist. A dutifully transgressive Futurist, he believed the arts should be liberated from the past – and therefore from the museums, galleries and concert halls – and performed instead in the streets, factories and workers' tenements. As for literature itself, the likes of Pushkin, Dostoyevsky and Tolstoy were fit only for the dustbin. There was a good deal of bluster and bravado in his stance.

Noting that bureaucrats and the bourgeoisie shore up their position by wielding the pen, he issues a clarion call to the writers of the Revolution: 'It is time / to fight back / with the pen. / It is time / to use the pen / to defend'. At stake is the rebuilding of the world along egalitarian lines. When he says that 'millions of future truths will grow / from our present-day sketches' he is speaking, not of abstract philosophical or political truths, but of individuals. The pen will proclaim them: 'long live / the red / worker's pen / our present-day weapon!' This is, of course, a long way from the truths of Seamus Heaney's squat pen, pensively digging for potatoes in the countryside.

Mayakovsky is obviously a prominent exemplar of the agitprop poet with a portfolio of messages to hand out; but he is also, no doubt, one of the great exponents of what we now call 'spoken word' poetry. Although he innovates on the printed page – the placing of the words, the breaking of the lines – we should also imagine his poems as reading scripts or even, better still, as after-the-fact reports of public performance. Taken in that manner, he would be a good model for today's young spoken-word artists who do not want simply to join the queue of colleagues delivering half-cooked, not to say half-baked, rap. For that purpose (and I have been reading some of them aloud), Womack works.

My main previous experience of Mayakovsky came by way of the three-volume *Selected Works* that Raduga Publishers issued in Moscow in 1985; variously translated, but mainly by Dorian Rottenberg. They are workmanlike versions, conveying little of the poet's sense of fun, except in rather starchy pantomime. Here is the last stanza of 'You!', as done by Rottenberg:

> To give up my life for the likes of you,
> lovers of woman-flesh, dinners and cars?
> I'd rather go and serve pineapple juice
> to the whores in Moscow's bars.

And here is James Womack's version of the same:

To give a life for you and yours,
you lovers of partridge and the pink trombone?
I'd rather be barman to a barful of whores,
serving them pineapple champagne!

I don't know the original – and there is surely a significant difference between lovers of 'woman-flesh' and those of 'the pink trombone' – but the tone here seems right. It fits with a Mayakovsky who is not only always eager to deliver, on his own terms but in the interests of the wider community, the shock of the new; but also happy to do so with a giggle and a shrug.

One of the shocks of the new was that it didn't have to be solemn – not, at least, until the authorities declared that it did. Womack does catch Mayakovsky's swagger and soul. His Mayakovsky tends to be more the spur-of-the-moment jester than the poster-boy of the Soviet state, as he posthumously became. (It was in 1935 that Stalin declared him the greatest poet of the Soviet era.) As a translator, Womack has great confidence in his control of Mayakovsky's variable tone, and also in the allusive resonance he allows himself, dodgy though it might sound to the purest of purists. For instance, he appears to quote David Bowie:

Oh you pretty things,
you people
who only worry about looking good when you dance …

And there is a distant echo of Ernie Wise which may be lost on younger readers.

Please don't
        ignore this note:
before firing off angry epistles
read the poem
        what I wrote.

Neither of these echoes tells us much about Mayakovsky or his times, even if they do deliver an internal chuckle. And here is Womack, taking viable liberties in the middle of the long poem 'Cloud in Trousers':

Wayne and Waynetta paint the town red,
pucker neanderthal brows –
but in their gob
the little corpses of most words lie dead.
Only two pull through:

'wanker'
and 'kebab'.

The original speaks of 'Krupps and Krupplets' (in Andrey Kneller's version, available online), a reference to the German family of arms manufacturers; so the choice of 'Wayne and Waynetta' is not exactly doing the whole of its job. (Their two animate words are, in Kneller's version, 'swine' and 'borsch'.) Clearly, Womack is willing to make certain sacrifices of historical context for the sake of the tone of voice.

Wayne and Waynetta Slob were grotesque characters created by Harry Enfield and Kathy Burke, in the early 1990s. 'Oh! You Pretty Things' was written by Bowie in 1971 for *Hunky Dory*. And the Ernie Wise line could come from anywhere in the 1960s or 1970s. These are dated resonances. Somewhat more in keeping with our times, the poem previously known as something like 'An Extraordinary Adventure Which Happened to Me, Vladimir Mayakovksy, in a Summer Cottage' becomes, in Womack's hands, a piece of online click-bait: 'Vladimir Mayakovsky Rented a Dacha One Summer; You Won't Believe What Happened Next'.

Also included here are a couple of the longer poems, 'Cloud in Trousers' and 'I Love', the 1913 play *Vladimir Mayakovsky*, and the 1926 film scenario *How's It Going?* (subtitled 'A Day in Five Cine-Details'). The shortest item, as fresh as on the day it was written, is the 1928 epigram:

> Productivity
>   and a living wage
> are recto and verso
>   of the same page.

Moments like this remind us that, setting aside my reservations about some of Womack's out-of-date updates, Mayakovsky can be both of-his-own-time and quite convincingly of ours too. The solutions on offer may have evolved in a century, but the basic injustices come in the same shape. Womack's brisk introduction to the book raises an interesting point:

> 'Between 1922 and 1928 Mayakovsky was the pre-eminent Soviet poet, moderating his style to meet an encroaching public philistinism. Perhaps he did not manage to become philistine enough. The last year or so of his life was marked by antagonism between him and his public, and in mid-April of 1930 Mayakovsky killed himself'.

It is sometimes hard to think of him as compromising with anyone in his more blustering verse – compromised, perhaps. But there is an inevitability about the process: the wider the audience, the greater the need to discard the egotism of artistic vision. Spoken-worders take heed.

Gregory Woods

Eat Your Pineapple

Eat your pineapple, chew your grouse:
your last day dawns, you bourgeois louse.

Vladimir Mayakovsky [1917]

---

from The Bureaucratiad

A concrete suggestion

I,
as you know,
am no manager or secretary.
I'm a poet with absolutely no bureaucratic capacity.
But I think
that it's necessary—
would be a mercy—
to take
the offices by the chimneys and give them a good shake.
And then to sit down
with the workers you'd shaken out,
and pick up just one of them,
and say to him:
'Write!'
With just one proviso,
a finishing touch:
'You go ahead, comrade, and write, *but not much*!'

[1922]

from Bastards!

'London.
A banquet.
Attended by kings and queens.
As a gesture, the guests' seats will not be golden.'

Damn you! God damn you all to hell!
I hope savages come from the colonies you conquered,
hungry and cannibal,
hunting your head
with its crown!
I hope your cities are burnt to the ground!
I hope the flame of rebellion burns
brightly over your kingdom!
I hope that—in copper cauldrons!—
your sons and heirs are boiled into jam!

[1922]

Spring

The snow is melted into drool.
The town's taken off its winter clothes.
Spring is here again, as foolish
and chatty as a sailor on shore leave.

[1918]

Danger of Death, Keep Out

John Le Carré, *A Legacy of Spies*, Viking/Penguin, 2017, 264 pages, hardback ISBN 9780241308547, £20

Perhaps we're all considerably wiser, or better informed, than we were when we first encountered the Le Carré universe of shabbiness, furtiveness, mendacity and callous ruthlessness that, fifty years ago or more, characterised his earliest novels and quintessentially, of course, *The Spy Who Came in from the Cold*.

We're no longer shocked by the scenes of atrocity that, deftly and without any gratuitous lingering, he places at the heart of his vision of the West's moral bankruptcy. When we journey, with Peter Guillam, the protagonist of *A Legacy of Spies*, to MI6's safe house in the New Forest and are introduced to 'the Submarine, a purpose-built isolation cell for instructing trainees in the unlovely arts of resisting and administering harsh interrogation … windowless padded walls, hand-to-foot manacles and head-splitting sound effects', we may be momentarily startled, but we recognise immediately its kinship with phenomena such as the CIA's black site torture room in Afghanistan, acknowledged by George W. Bush in September 2006 and claimed as essential to the containment of Islamic fundamentalism, with rendition, waterboarding and Guantanamo Bay.

We recognise also – le Carré has spent decades, from *The Little Drummer Girl* onwards, persuading us to engage imaginatively with systems of exploitation, profiteering and criminality which are global in their reach – that the narrow struggle for ideological supremacy conducted by Smiley, Guillam and the ancient clan of Cold War operatives, now rising once more from the dead, never constituted a world apart, or one that was immune from a much wider culpability.

Robert McCrumb in *The Guardian* (September 2016) is therefore right to detect a deep-seated pessimism in the current novel's immediate precursor, Le Carré's memoir *The Pigeon Tunnel*, when it comes to assessing legacies. On the one hand, there's the recognition that old, discredited regimes survive revolution and war and go on functioning in, or infiltrating, new realities (the Nazis in post-war Germany, Communists in the Soviet Empire and present day Russia, countless examples across the other continents of murderous regimes propped up indefinitely by superpower self-interest), as do intelligence services – 'like the wiring in a house: the new owner moves in, he drops the switch, and it's the same old lights that come on again'. Worse still, perhaps, for Le Carré personally is the British Establishment's propensity to mythologise its own history so cavalierly it constitutes, among spy services, 'a class apart'. Le Carré takes aim, with withering scorn, both at the organisation's atrocious operational record and at its readiness, whenever necessary, to collude with barbarism: 'wasn't my former Service energetically trading intelligence with the Gestapo right up to 1939? Wasn't it on friendly terms with Muammar Gaddafi's chief of secret police right up to the last days of Gaddafi's rule?'

Where McCrumb gets it wrong is in underestimating the vehemence in this passage, and others like it, and characterising the author of *The Pigeon Tunnel* as a 'slightly chastened figure, all passion spent'. Nor should we miss the many instances of individual heroism Le Carré pays tribute to in the course of his reminiscences: Sakharov, Vadim Bakatin, Oldrich Cerny, Salah Tamari, Yvette Pierpaoli, above all 'the striving and endurance of so-called ordinary people who weren't ordinary at all'.

In *A Legacy of Spies*, what astonishes most of all is the redoubled narrative energy with which an octogenarian novelist conducts what may be his ultimate counterattack on behalf of those with the will to resist. As ever, the pigeon tunnel is stocked with victims. As ever, innocence and systemic brutality perform their grisly, voyeuristically compelling dance of death. Fallow deer add to the New Forest hideaway's 'air of cultivated charm and tranquillity' a few steps away from a corpse hanging from a tree by a thread of nylon - one thinks, with revulsion, of the fate of David Kelly. When we're told a character is 'neurotic but extremely controlled, and highly vulnerable' or 'sweet ... humanity breathes out of him', we wait for the noose of political expediency to tighten.

In an Orwellian context of maximum surveillance, the barest expressions of human identity – desire, protectiveness, solidarity, *love* (the equivalent of Alec Leamas going back for the already murdered Liz at the Berlin Wall in *The Spy*) – court catastrophe and, predictably, women and children come off worst. Le Carré pulls the whole story forward into a contemporary setting in which the front line perpetrators, in this case including Peter Guillam, themselves face court proceedings in a cosmetic exercise designed to shore up the Service's lack of genuine accountability. The odds are stacked against them, against truth, against any kind of moral reckoning. The 'gruesome bastion' on the Thames at Vauxhall – Le Carré's contempt is palpable – with its malevolent apparatchiks, its Bunnys and Lauras – has little to fear, it believes, from antequated spooks on the verge of extinction such as 'Millie McCraig's motionless shadow looking down on me from the window' of Smiley's defunct operational centre 'The Stables', or Jim Prideaux still out to grass in the dilapidated caravan of *Tinker, Tailor, Soldier, Spy*.

But Smiley and Guillam in particular, the consummate hangman and the consummate philanderer, have both had their Damascene moments on the road to a reclaimed humanity. It's given to Guillam to spell out the ethical conundrum any legacy worth handing down must find an answer to: 'how much of our human feeling can we dispense with in the name of freedom ... before we cease to feel either human or free?' And it's Smiley, the knight with the rueful countenance, who sets off in pursuit of his former employers, armed with the documentary evidence that will unmask them. Perhaps the children Leamas remembers in his last conscious moment 'waving cheerfully through the window' of a car on the autobahn, their lives miraculously spared, symbolise a future worth dying for, after all.

Stephen Winfield

Austerity's re-working

Vickie Cooper and David Whyte (editors), *The Violence of Austerity*, Pluto Press, 2017, 256 pages, paperback ISBN 9780745399485, £16.99

At the turn of the century, an obscure Home Office poster was discovered in Barter Books, a shop in Alnwick, Northumberland, with the motivational slogan 'Keep Calm and Carry On'. It had been prepared in 1939 for use in case of a coastal invasion by the Nazis, and was designed to steady the national nerves in the face of such a calamitous event. The poster was never used in these circumstances but became a fashionable, ironic, comedy catchphrase after its unearthing in 2000. The phrase adorns mugs, t-shirts, key-rings, fridge magnets, bags, tea towels, pencil cases and, of course, posters, and has cultivated an industry fuelled by post-war nostalgia. It's a powerful image of a clichéd yet outmoded expression of 'traditional' English stoicism, of British pluck, of stiff upper lip, and it is a gloriously kitsch memento of determined resolve in the face of hardship. This nostalgia for remaining positive in the face of adversity provided an easily identifiable and artistic backdrop to the 'age of austerity' that the UK entered following the financial crisis of 2007/8. We were told by the media and successive governments to 'Keep Calm and Carry On', to 'make do and mend' and that 'we are all in this together'.

Such a comradely, belt-tightening narrative set the stage for ensuring that the necessity of austerity measures was clear, and provided an historical lens through which we were asked to cope with them. We were told that the deficit accrued from the bailout of the banks was actually a result of public and personal profligacy: we had collectively spent too much. Successive Labour governments had overspent on the public sector, handing out gold-plated pensions to public servants and dishing out welfare to anyone who filled out the necessary forms. In turn, we, the public, had gone overboard by purchasing as many consumer goods as we could possibly acquire on credit. In short, the financial crisis was represented as stemming from a combination of government recklessness and debt-fuelled consumption. Despite no hard data to support the idea that government overspending caused the deficit, the only way out of the economic mess was to cut back. From this perspective, austerity is viewed as a purely economic procedure that comes down to nothing more than the fiscal need to cut the deficit and slash public spending. This view that was put forth as the rationale for austerity in the UK, which included freezing Child Benefit and public sector wages, reducing housing benefits, implementing the 'Bedroom Tax', and introducing Personal Independence Payments, to name but a few measures. However, it was the façade of togetherness that, as *The Violence of Austerity* demonstrates, 'played a key part in the ideological making of austerity' by organising consent for the cuts and simultaneously deflected blame from the private sector and banks.

The politics of austerity not only has a scarcely hidden ideological dimension, in that it was framed as the common sense and only way to pay for the massive increase in public debt caused by the financial crisis, it also has a deeply nefarious dimension that is kept from public scrutiny. In *The Violence of Austerity*, editors Vickie Cooper and David Whyte draw together research that collectively presents evidence of the 'violent consequences of government policy conducted in the name of "austerity".' Together, the 24 articles expose austerity as a process of cuts to publicly funded services that has led to policies that target the most vulnerable in society. These cuts are implemented through various bureaucracies and institutions that make each policy a reality and routinise the harmful effects of deciding whether, for example, someone is legally homeless or fit for work. In four sections the contributors examine in detail the impacts that workfare, the asylum system, fuel poverty, homelessness, and work capability assessments (WCA) have on the mental and physical health of hundreds of thousands of people in the United Kingdom.

Benefit sanctions feature in both the workfare scheme and WCA measures, and underpin the rise of food bank usage, food and fuel poverty and homelessness. The impact that such sanctions have on individuals is evidenced by the shocking stories related throughout *The Violence of Austerity*. In his chapter on 'Welfare Reforms and the Attack on Disabled People', John Pring charts the series of brutal cuts to disabled people's support as Personal Independence Payments (PIP) slowly replaced the Disability Living Allowance (DLA) from 2013 onwards. One impact of this cut was that 'by July 2016 up to 700 disabled people a week who had previously claimed DLA were being forced to hand back their Motability vehicles'. There were more cuts to come, as eligibility for the out-of-work disability benefit, Employment and Support Allowance (ESA), began to be assessed through the work capability assessments. These assessments, delivered by private companies (Atos from 2008 and Maximus from 2015), determined whether an ESA claimant was fit for work. However, it was discovered that in a number of cases these private assessors had not sought evidence of illness from GPs, psychiatrists or clinical psychologists, resulting in people being forced back into work when they were not well enough. Pring recounts one notable incident, the case of Andrew Davidson, whose coroner's report stated that his 'decision to take his own life had been triggered by being found "fit to work".' As the article goes on to show, Davidson's case is not an outlier, with one study showing that thousands of people have died not long after being found 'fit for work'. More worrying still is the evidence that, even if you are 'lucky' enough to be offered Employment and Support Allowance, there is the constant threat of benefit sanctions that are regularly implemented without the prior knowledge of the recipient. One anonymous welfare rights officer tells us:

> 'Frequently clients do not know that they've been sanctioned until they don't receive their benefit. They've received no letter and given no information on the right to appeal ... Clients have told me they are shoplifting to eat.'

Such punitive measures has led to the formation of Disabled People Against Cuts (DPAC), set up to 'fight the austerity-driven erosion of disabled people's living conditions and human rights'. Another grassroots organisation that campaigns against the impact of austerity on benefit claimants is Boycott Workfare. This group aims to expose the violence of the workfare scheme and to 'end forced unpaid work for people who receive welfare'. In essence, workfare means people are sent on compulsory work placements *or* have their Job Seekers Allowance taken away. In their contribution, Jon Burnett and David Whyte analyse the testimonies of more than 500 people who logged on to Boycott Workfare's website. The analysis revealed that working environments in some of the organisations that had signed up to the government's scheme were almost Dickensian in practice. Claimants reported being 'expected to complete physical labour at an intense pace,' were afforded no breaks, some mentioned that they had to pay for access to the toilets, and many reported having their illnesses ignored by employers. Not only were people forced to work at an unhealthy rate but, in several cases, they were also working in unsafe and often illegal conditions. Alarmingly, the employers with the highest number of abuses included charities or social enterprises.

The picture of austerity Britain painted by this important book stands in stark contrast to the image painted by successive governments since the crash. The financial crisis may have started as an economic problem to be solved, but it was ideologically reworked into the political problem of how to allocate blame and responsibility. This ideological reworking focused on the claimed profligacy of government spending on public services and welfare – a narrative that was assisted by the negative image of welfare that reassured workers that those on benefits were 'feeling the pinch too', that 'we were all in this together', and that we needed to Keep Calm and Carry On. What *The Violence of Austerity* clearly articulates is that the consequence of this reworking is the de-politicising and normalising of a number of increasingly punitive measures that have a harmful, and in some cases, fatal effect on people and their lives. It exposes and confronts the impact of austerity and highlights the work of a diverse body of activist and campaigning groups who tirelessly challenge the government, its policies and the institutions that implement them, in the courts and on the street.

Abigail Rhodes

Brexit slobber

Written and illustrated by Madeleina Kay, *Theresa Maybe in Brexitland*, 2017, 56 pages large format, paperback ISBN 9780995707412, £5

Madeleina Kay won the 'EU in My Region' blogging competition and duly made her first visit to Brussels to attend a European Commission journalism course. She dressed as Supergirl, and caught the eye of the world's press whilst sitting quietly at the front of the room where Michel Barnier and David Davis were about to give a press conference at the end of round five of their dogged negotiations. Madeleina was accredited for her visit to the Commission Press Centre, but made no fuss when she was asked to leave prior to the press conference starting. 'They thought I might pull a stunt like the guy who gave Theresa May a P45 at the Tory Party Conference,' she later told the BBC.

A fearless young activist and European citizen, Supergirl held her copy of *Theresa Maybe in Brexitland* for the assembled photographers and television cameras to see. The Superhero's mission is to save Britain from the emerging horrors of Brexitland. In bright colours and large readable type, her Lewis Caroll inspired political satire 'parallels the story of British politics following the Brexit vote'. In all this vital work, Supergirl is helped by Alba White Wolf, her elegant Alsatian companion:

> 'An enormous white wolf was looking down at her with large eyes, and cautiously stretching out one paw, trying to touch the Brexit. The white wolf sniffed the Brexit as though it were filled with delicious biscuits. It gave Theresa Maybe a big lick covering her head in slobber, but she didn't seem to mind because the white wolf was such a friendly creature.' *www.albawhitewolf.com*

TS